# Praise for *Great Myths of Aging*

"A good read for everyone who wants a balanced and accessible summary of the current scientific evidence on aspects of aging of most concern to people's everyday lives."

*Professor Elizabeth A. Maylor, University of Warwick*

"An engaging read, this book will reassure the older and educate the younger. Myth-busting at its playful, informative best."

*Michael S. North, Postdoctoral Research Scientist, Columbia University, Susan T. Fiske, Eugene Higgins Professor of Psychology and Professor of Public Affairs, Princeton University*

"This book will be a service to teachers and students, but equally so to middle-aged and older adults in helping them make life decisions based on the best information. Readers will find quite a few surprises and some comfort about aging."

*David J. Ekerdt, Professor of Sociology, University of Kansas*

"Given the continuing interest in making aging research available not only to professionals and policymakers but also to laypersons, Joan Erber and Lenore Szuchman have provided a valuable service by addressing a topic of great social significance. In this highly readable volume these authors aim to dispel the myths about aging and older adulthood by drawing upon up-to-date research and scholarship from disciplines such as gerontology, psychology, sociology, and communication. I enjoyed reading it, and recommend it to you."

*Chandra M. Mehrotra, Professor of Psychology, The College of St. Scholastica*

# Great Myths of Psychology

**Series Editors**
Scott O. Lilienfeld
Steven Jay Lynn

This superb series of books tackles a host of fascinating myths and misconceptions regarding specific domains of psychology, including child development, aging, marriage, brain science, and mental illness, among many others. Each book not only dispels multiple erroneous but widespread psychological beliefs, but provides readers with accurate and up-to-date scientific information to counter them. Written in engaging, upbeat, and user-friendly language, the books in the myths series are replete with scores of intriguing examples drawn from everyday psychology. As a result, readers will emerge from each book entertained and enlightened. These unique volumes will be invaluable additions to the bookshelves of educated laypersons interested in human nature, as well as of students, instructors, researchers, journalists, and mental health professionals of all stripes.

www.wiley.com/go/psychmyths

## Published

50 Great Myths of Popular Psychology
*Scott O. Lilienfeld, Steven Jay Lynn, John Ruscio, and Barry L. Beyerstein*

Great Myths of Aging
*Joan T. Erber and Lenore T. Szuchman*

Great Myths of the Brain
*Christian Jarrett*

## Forthcoming

Great Myths of Child Development
*Steven Hupp and Jeremy Jewell*

Great Myths of Intimate Relations
*Matthew D. Johnson*

Great Myths of Personality
*M. Brent Donnellan and Richard E. Lucas*

Great Myths of Autism
*James D. Herbert*

Great Myths of Education and Learning
*Jeffrey D. Holmes and Aaron S. Richmond*

50 Great Myths of Popular Psychology, Second Edition
*Scott O. Lilienfeld, Steven Jay Lynn, John Ruscio, and Barry L. Beyerstein*

# GREAT MYTHS
# OF AGING

### Joan T. Erber
### and
### Lenore T. Szuchman

## WILEY Blackwell

For Lauren, Isaac, Megan, Rebecca,
Eli, Reuben, Ida, Noa, and Sadie

We hope they will not entertain myths about
their aging grandmas

# CONTENTS

# ACKNOWLEDGMENTS

First and foremost, we are indebted to Scott Lilienfeld and Steven Lynn for inviting us to contribute to this series. Their encouragement provided momentum, and their detailed suggestions and guidance along the way were indispensable.

We are grateful to the folks at Wiley Blackwell who helped us bring this book to fruition. Senior Editor Matt Bennett's enthusiasm for the project and for our potential to make a valuable contribution to the *Myths* series gave us the impetus to prepare the proposal. Danielle Descoteaux, Senior Acquisitions Editor, took over the project and guided us with kindness and insight. Her assistant, Olivia Wells, and Senior Project Editor Karen Shield supported us in many ways, and Production Editor Tom Bates, together with the entire production team, were invaluable in the publication of this book. We also thank the anonymous reviewers of our early book proposal who made excellent suggestions that helped us tweak the final myths list.

Dr. Stephen Konscol shared his expertise on changes in conceptualizing some types of pathology as *DSM-IV-TR* gave way to *DSM-5*. The following friends and relatives offered suggestions on media sources that perpetuate many of the myths that we have attempted to bust: Bill Gibson, Carolyn Sobel, Jane Spirn, Elliott Stein, and Jeff Szuchman. Thanks also to Mark Szuchman for offering some very helpful editorial comments throughout the many hours Joan and Lenore were collaborating by phone. Finally, we appreciate our friends and acquaintances of all ages who shared their views on aging and older adulthood.

# INTRODUCTION

If you ask people you know well, or even people you barely know at all, to voice their opinions on various aspects of aging and older adulthood, they will probably be more than happy to do so. One thing is certain: most people already have strongly held views on this topic. As we were writing this book, we mentioned its title (*Great Myths of Aging*) to close friends, casual friends, and even people we had just met for the first time. These people ranged in age – some were young adults, some were middle-aged, and some were already members of what most of us consider to be the older adult age group (65+). In every instance, people were eager to weigh in with their thoughts on a broad swath of subjects related to the aging process, and particularly their thoughts about older adults in general. Indeed, most considered themselves to be experts on these topics. But when it came right down to it, their avowed expertise often rested on personal experience, anecdotal evidence, or both. We have no gripe with personal experience; we, too, commonly speak from such a vantage point. However, in the area of our *professional* expertise, we are partial to the scientific method – which can often lead to very different conclusions. If good science contradicts a single personal experience or two, then we advocate that people vote with science. After all, we would all want others to shape their approach toward us in a way that is informed by the best and most valid sources rather than on the basis of personal opinions.

Before delving into specific myths that circulate about aging and older adults, let's start by discussing what we mean by *myths*. One definition refers to a traditional story that explains some phenomenon – such as the Greek myths we all studied in school. These are understood to be cultural

*Great Myths of Aging*, First Edition. Joan T. Erber and Lenore T. Szuchman.
© 2015 John Wiley & Sons, Inc. Published 2015 by John Wiley & Sons, Inc.

beliefs, perhaps at odds with science, but often useful in their own right. For example, they often provide powerful and lasting moral lessons. However, these are not the kind of myths that "mythbusters" tackle.

Another definition of myth is a belief that is patently false, and this can actually be downright harmful. In this book we will try to persuade you that some common beliefs about older people are just plain wrong and can lead to lost opportunities for keeping some of the most experienced and productive members of society involved in the social fabric.

At age 93, Roger Angell, a long-time editor of the *New Yorker*, wrote a moving essay about his experience with aging, entitled "This Old Man: Life in the Nineties." Although most of his views are decidedly upbeat, he does remind us of the harm that some of these views can inflict. For example, in a conversation with old friends, who themselves are in their 60s, he begins to feel invisible:

> There's a pause, and I chime in with a couple of sentences. The others look at me politely, then resume the talk exactly at the point where they've just left it. What? Hello? Didn't I just say something? Have I left the room? I didn't expect to take over the chat but did await a word or two of response. Not tonight, though. (Women I know say that this began to happen to them when they passed 50.) When I mention the phenomenon to anyone around my age, I get back nods and smiles. Yes, we're invisible. Honored, respected, even loved, but not quite worth listening to anymore. (Angell, 2014, February 17 & 24, p. 63)

There are a number of myths to explain why folks might begin to ignore older people in conversation, and we touch on some in this book. For example. some people might assume that older adults aren't keeping up with modern life (stuck in their ways) and don't know much about the topic at hand, that they aren't likely to be accurate in their statements (losing brain power), or that they can't hear too well and it is effortful to speak loudly and clearly to make them understand.

When we argue that certain beliefs about older adults are clearly erroneous, we present scientific evidence to back up our position. In this way, we consider ourselves to be mythbusters. But are all myths based on information that is completely fallacious? Perhaps someone has had a specific experience with an older family member. Or possibly a person is having his or her own encounter with the aging process. If people have definite ideas based on what seems to be happening to someone close to them or in their own lives, we cannot very well deny them their opinions, which were obviously formed in part as the result of personal experience. However, there is little doubt that myths about aging can be erroneous simply because they are overgeneralizations that are based on individualized circumstances. Such circumstances may be personally salient but certainly do not always apply to all, or even to the majority of, older adults. We will do some mythbusting by providing evidence that many myths cannot and, in most circumstances should not, be broadly applied.

Although there are some exceptions, myths about aging and older adulthood tend to be negative (anti-aging) rather than positive (pro-aging). Young and middle-aged adults may be fearful about uncertain and potentially unpleasant possibilities, which, as is the nature of myths, get magnified and generalized. Indeed, a web search on "aging stereotypes" yields a plethora of hits about grouchy, frumpy, and smelly old folks. Thus, our myths include some of these overgeneralizations (e.g., the idea that all older adults need diapers and older women don't care about their looks) in addition to some beliefs that are flat-out wrong (e.g., older adults get into more auto accidents than young adults). However, we have not overlooked the pro-aging myths (e.g., older people are all wise), although, frankly, these are in the minority.

At this juncture it is important to remind our readers of two obvious points: Of all the stigmatized groups we know of, the older adult age group (a) is the only group that every person will join, assuming a long enough life; and (b) is likely to include people whom we love and care about. By themselves, these are good enough reasons to study the basis for the myths we will discuss. Understanding that a belief is really a myth should ultimately lower the influence it has on our thinking.

Many "myths" in this book are really stereotypes about aging and older adulthood, which are more often negative than positive in Western countries. In an excellent overview of age stereotypes, Staudinger and Bowen (2010) point out that negative age stereotypes begin as early as childhood. School-aged children often have negative expectations of older adults, and these are bound to affect their interpersonal interactions with older people. The authors contend that stereotypes about older people can have two major harmful effects: "(a) The social environment reinforces behaviors in older adults that conform with the stereotype and (b) the older person internalizes the old-age stereotype" (p. 281).

Stereotypes can result in self-fulfilling prophecies, and research by Becca Levy and her colleagues bears this out. In one study (Levy, 1996), older adults were implicitly primed with exposure either to words designed to elicit a negative age stereotype (e.g., decline, dependent, senile, confused) or to words designed to elicit a positive stereotype (e.g., wise, alert, sage, learned). In an implicit priming experiment, words are shown so quickly that participants do not consciously perceive them. In this case, older adult participants were instructed to localize the word/flash of light on a screen by pressing a key. They were not consciously aware that actual words had even been shown. Yet the older adults who were implicitly primed with negative words did more poorly on a subsequent memory test compared with older adults who were implicitly primed with positive words. Levy, Zonderman, Slade, and Ferrucci (2012) demonstrated that negative self-stereotypes can have far-reaching negative effects on memory even 38 years into the future. Those who held negative age stereotypes at earlier ages, especially when they thought those stereotypes were relevant to themselves, performed more poorly on memory tests many years later compared to those who held less negative age stereotypes.

Levy, Slade, Kunkel, and Kasl (2002) demonstrated that negative beliefs about one's own aging are related to health outcomes such as greater cardiovascular response to stress. In a relatively recent report (Levy, Zonderman, Slade & Ferrucci, 2009), individuals aged 49 and younger who held negative age stereotypes about aging were more likely to experience a cardiovascular event in the 38 years that followed compared with individuals who held positive stereotypes about aging earlier in life. Thus "age stereotypes internalized earlier in life can have a far-reaching effect on health" (p. 297). It is conceivable that poor health earlier in life influences a person's view about aging as well as the probability of cardiovascular problems later on. However, it seems clear that the way people view older adults and the way older adults view themselves can have a broad array of influences on functioning in later life. Staudinger and Bowen (2010) argue that negative stereotypes about old age can ultimately limit older adults' opportunities for personal growth, preventing them from achieving their potential.

In this book, we present evidence that serves to "bust" each myth. To achieve our goal, we relied on studies published in academic journals and academic books written by recognized authorities. We also incorporated information from national media such as the *New York Times*, which often publishes articles and essays that relate to cultural trends. Many of these articles include interviews with professionals involved in ongoing studies on topics related to aging and older adulthood. We also scoured the web – where we found a great deal of up-to-date survey research, made available by groups such as the Pew Research Center and AARP. In addition, we obtained census information related to the myths from government websites.

We have divided the myths into five basic categories: the body, the mind, the self, living contexts, and endings and loss. The Body concerns the physical changes that occur with age. For example, it contains myths about the type of hearing loss that most commonly develops with age and the ways in which both speakers and listeners can adjust to it. We also cover myths on the negative stereotypes about locomotion, such as whether older adults actually should be worried about falling down and whether everyone else should worry about older people spending time behind the wheel. Finally, we take on the taboo about sex. We note that older people are undeservedly considered sexless in our culture, and we argue that part of the reason is that the young consider the sex lives of the old as just too disgusting to contemplate. This disturbing opinion deserves attention.

Many myths about the Mind are about forgetfulness and diseases such as Alzheimer's, which affect cognitive function. There are fine-grained distinctions to be made concerning the mild types of decline that can be expected with typical aging and the various symptoms and potential treatments for a variety of diseases that are associated with cognitive symptoms. It is here also that we examine one of the positive myths: wisdom comes naturally with age. Regretfully, we will need to debunk this one too.

The category of Self relates to personality. Our society attributes a number of negative traits to older adults, such as being stingy and grouchy, that do not hold up to scrutiny. It is interesting to note that traits that are probably life-long in most people who exhibit them have become associated only with old age. In this section we also consider the problem of how a foreshortened future affects personality. We explain that older people are not necessarily depressed about their age and that they still see themselves as having a future in which they can fulfill some of their hopes and dreams. Likewise, because the future is viable (although finite), therapy can be just as useful for improving that future as it can when the future seems to stretch out infinitely.

Next, in Living Contexts, we consider the social environment that older adults inhabit in our culture. There is some positive stereotyping in how we see grandparenting; again, regretfully, we must bust some pro-aging myths here. On the negative side are the myths about retirement: the presumed decline in work-related skills and the depressing fact of being put out to pasture when retirement occurs.

Finally, we present end-of-life issues. What happens when a husband dies and his widow still craves a social life? Who in our society is most afraid of death? Where do people die? We have found plenty of misperceptions related to these questions.

We hope that this book leads to spirited discussion on topics about which most people have a keen interest. We feel quite certain that every reader has family members who are approaching or have already entered their late years. And, of course, we hope that all of our readers can themselves experience a productive aging process and a long, high-quality life. If we are lucky, we will all have an opportunity to do so.

# 1 THE BODY

## "Speak up! I can't hear you!"

Sometimes it does seem as if older people are all hard of hearing. When people can't hear, they may ask to have things repeated a lot or they may tune out and become uninvolved in conversation. Younger relatives end

*Great Myths of Aging*, First Edition. Joan T. Erber and Lenore T. Szuchman.
© 2015 John Wiley & Sons, Inc. Published 2015 by John Wiley & Sons, Inc.

up shouting to try to make themselves heard, and they can lose patience when the older people won't try hearing aids. Younger people may over-react to the stereotype of the hard-of-hearing older person by "talking down" to all older people. In one survey of 84 people over age 60, 39% reported that they had been patronized or talked down to at least once (Palmore, 2001).

It is true that certain types of hearing loss are typically part of the "normal" aging process, but shouting is not usually the solution. It is also true that there are barriers for some people to getting hearing aids, but stubbornness is rarely one of them. Yet the myth persists. For example, a press release about a University of Florida study on the effects of hearing loss in older adults explicitly mentions the stereotype of older adults as being stubborn about admitting hearing loss. In this section we discuss the effects of the type of hearing loss that is typical of aging, and the best way to speak to someone who has this problem. We also evaluate the most likely reasons people might have for not purchasing hearing aids.

## Myth #1   It is best to speak to an older person as you would to a small child – loudly, slowly, and with exaggerated emphasis

There is little doubt that changes in hearing trouble a large proportion of older adults. Hearing loss is among the most common conditions associated with aging. It affects approximately 18% of adults aged 45 to 64, 30% of adults aged 65 to 74, and 47% of adults 75 years and older (National Institute on Deafness and Other Communication Disorders, National Institutes of Health, 2010).

The type of age-related hearing loss characteristic of most individuals as they grow older is called *presbycusis*. It can come on so gradually that older adults do not necessarily notice any decline in their hearing. Perhaps for that reason, they are not always ready to admit they have a hearing loss, blaming any difficulty they experience on the acoustics of the room or the fact that the speaker is whispering.

When people, especially younger adults, assume that older adults cannot hear very well, they do what comes naturally: they speak louder, and when that doesn't work, they shout. Increasing the volume of speech may be helpful up to a point. Unfortunately, if the volume is too high, there is generally little gain. In fact, increasing the volume of speech beyond a reasonable level often backfires because it can actually distort the spoken message. Older adults may say, "I hear it but I cannot understand it," which illustrates a phenomenon called *phonemic regression.*

With presbycusis, there is typically greater difficulty associated with high-frequency than with low-frequency tones. Women's voices usually have higher frequencies than men's voices. For this reason, older adults typically hear men better than they hear women. Also, within the range of human speech, consonants such as *f, t, th, s,* and *z* are characterized by high frequency, so it is not surprising that older adults have difficulty discriminating among words with high-frequency consonants (e.g., "fit" and "sit"). If frequency rather than volume is the problem, increasing the volume will not be as effective as lowering the frequency. One way to do that would be to reword the message, substituting key words that minimize high-frequency consonants. Also, women can make an effort to drop their voices to a lower pitch rather than increase the volume.

Here is another issue related to hearing loss in older adults: processing language takes time on a central (brain) level, and there is slowing with age in cognitive processing. To some extent, slowing down the pace of speech can be beneficial. But if the pace is so slow that it does not conform to the natural flow of language, slowing down is not usually helpful (Kemper, 1994; Wingfield & Stine-Morrow, 2000).

Prosody is an aspect of speech that refers to emphasis. People are known to use what has been termed *motherese* when speaking to small children. Motherese is characterized by exaggerated prosody, as well as by an unnaturally high-pitched tone often coupled with terms of endearment (e.g., *honey, sweetie, dear*). When directed toward older adults, this type of speech has been termed *elderspeak.* Elderspeak is characterized not only by shortened sentences, simplified grammar, and slower speech, but also by exaggerated pitch and intonation (exaggerated prosody).

Kemper and Harden (1999) set out to determine which characteristics of elderspeak are beneficial for older adult listeners and which may not be. They had older adults watch and listen to a videotape of a speaker who was describing a route while also tracing it on a map. The older adults reported that instructions were easier to follow when the speaker reduced the grammatical complexity of the instructions (that is, minimized the number of subordinated and embedded clauses) and when the speaker used semantic elaboration (that is, repeated and expanded upon what was said). (Note that the sentence you just read is pretty complex in that way.) If the speaker used simpler grammar and semantic elaboration, older adults improved their accuracy when they had to reproduce the same route on a map of their own. In contrast, cutting the length of the speaker's sentences did not improve their comprehension of the instructions, nor did it improve their performance when they traced a map of their own. Also, older listeners did not find it helpful when the speaker spoke at an unnaturally slow rate with many pauses or with exaggerated prosody. In short, being spoken to at a slower than normal speed and in atypically short phrases, as well as with exaggerated pitch and intonation, does little to enhance older adults' ability to comprehend speech.

Furthermore, even though typically well-intentioned, using elderspeak may not be a nice thing to do. Ryan and her colleagues (Ryan, Anas, & Gruneir, 2006; Ryan, Hummert, & Boich, 1995) contend that exaggerated prosody and terms of endearment are patronizing and often lead to a "communication predicament" situation: older adults feel uncomfortable when speakers use this manner of speech, so they prefer to withdraw altogether from any communicative interaction.

In sum, communication with older adults who have typical age-related hearing loss is most satisfactory when the language used by the speaker has reasonable volume but is not too loud. Speech should not be overly fast, but it should be no slower than the natural flow of the language and should minimize the use of high-frequency key words. It is also helpful if the speakers' sentences are not too grammatically complex and if the speaker states the message in several different ways (elaborates). Finally, it is important for speakers to face older adult listeners, who can then take advantage of visual cues such as reading the speaker's lips and seeing the speaker's body language. If it becomes clear that an older listener does not understand a message, changing the wording will probably be more effective than increasing the volume, slowing down speech to a snail's pace, or using exaggerated prosody. And elderspeak is related to baby talk, so it can be offensive.

## Myth #2 Hearing aids are beneficial for older adults in just about any situation, but many are just too stubborn to use them

There is little question that as people grow older, they experience changes in both vision and hearing. People do not seem to be ambivalent about wearing eyeglasses to correct their vision, nor do they hesitate to visit an eye-care specialist for a change in prescription that will improve their visual acuity. Yet as many as 22.9 million older Americans have a hearing loss but do not own or use a hearing aid (Chien & Lin, 2012). Lin, Thorpe, Gordon-Salant, and Ferrucci (2011) estimate that only approximately one-fifth of older adults with hearing loss use a hearing aid.

Popelka et al. (1998) conducted a study on 1,629 Wisconsin residents ranging in age from 48 to 92, all of whom had a hearing loss, to determine the extent to which they made use of hearing aids. Only 14.6% used hearing aids. Furthermore, among a subset of the study participants with severe hearing loss, the prevalence of hearing-aid use was only 55%. A number of participants reported that they owned a hearing aid but no longer used it. This problem is not confined to the U.S. A large-scale study was conducted in Australia on hearing-aid use among 3,000 individuals aged 49 to 99, with an average age of 67 (Hartley, Rochtchina, Newall, Golding, & Mitchell, 2010). Although 33% of the participants had a hearing loss, only 11% owned a hearing aid. Of those who did own a hearing aid, 24% reported that they never used it.

Given that hearing loss is a frequent occurrence among the older population, why are older adults not lining up to get hearing aids? The myth is that they are just too stubborn to do so. But according to Lin et al. (2011), older adults, and indeed people in general, tend to undervalue the negative impact of hearing loss not only on the ability to communicate but also potentially on health and general well-being. In fact, in a survey of 240 people who had no sight or hearing deficits, approximately three-quarters would prefer to lose hearing rather than sight (Kim, Goldman, & Biederman, 2008).

Age-related hearing difficulties usually come on gradually and insidiously, so many people do not realize that their hearing has declined until the loss is significant. Older adults may complain that other people are mumbling, that there is something wrong with the acoustics (sound system) in a movie theater or playhouse, and so on. They often deny that the problem lies with their own hearing capability, which could well be a reason for their low rate of hearing-aid use.

At some point, however, hearing loss can become sufficiently severe that older adults are no longer able to deny it and are forced to recognize that their hearing difficulties are not solely attributable to other people's mumbling or poor environmental acoustics. Also, other people (often family members) start to broach the subject of hearing impairment with the older adults. Then why do many older adults who could benefit from a hearing aid not get one?

Before assuming it is just stubbornness that prevents older adults from obtaining and/or using a hearing aid, it is important to recognize that there are a number of other reasons. First, getting and/or wearing a hearing aid is likely to signify to people that they are growing older, certainly more so than is the case with eyeglasses, which are worn by people of all ages. This means that failure to get a hearing aid could stem from denial about aging. In addition, some older adults may feel that wearing a hearing aid would make them look "stupid," and would signify that they are incompetent. In short, wearing a hearing aid is a threat to their self-image (Ryan, Hummert, & Anas, 1997, November). This fear is not completely unfounded, given the existence of ageism in the U.S. as well as other countries (e.g., Belgium, Costa Rica, Hong Kong, Japan, Israel, and South Korea), wherein older adults are considered to be sweet and warm, but feeble (Cuddy, Norton, & Fiske, 2005).

Failure to get or use a hearing aid for fear of being considered incompetent could well be a reason for the low rate of hearing-aid use among older adults. But nowadays, many people wear an earpiece to talk on the phone or listen to music. Also, many modern hearing aids are very small and can be reasonably well hidden. Even so, small hearing aids can be extremely costly for older adults living on limited budgets and may also be difficult to manipulate. Larger, less expensive ones may not look so "hip."

Another reason for older adults' low rate of hearing-aid use could be that it takes careful evaluation by ear, nose, and throat specialists and/or audiologists to determine whether a person with a specific type of hearing loss will benefit from a hearing aid. And when a hearing aid could help, it must be carefully tailored to a person's hearing loss. A hearing aid that amplifies all frequencies (even ones for which the wearer has relatively normal hearing) will be uncomfortable and probably not very useful. Many people try several hearing aids before they find one that works well for them (National Institute on Deafness and Other Communication Disorders, National Institutes of Health, 2001). Once again, there is the expense – hearing aids custom-made for an individual's specific hearing loss are costly and not covered by health insurance. Furthermore, hearing-aid owners do not just walk out the door after purchasing a hearing aid. Rather, they must be counseled on how to operate a hearing aid to achieve the maximum benefit. Popelka et al. (1998) suggest that to best deal with barriers to hearing-aid use, it may be necessary for hearing-aid professionals to offer users a long-term program of ongoing support and counseling.

Unlike eyeglasses, which can be prescribed to correct vision across a variety of situations, hearing aids may not be beneficial in every situation. Older hearing aids had limited usefulness in environments with background noise, such as restaurants with clattering dishes and multiple conversations going on (Schneider & Pichora-Fuller, 2000). Some older adults may have tried those in the past and become too frustrated to try the newer generation of hearing aids, which are better at reducing background noise. Also, expense is an issue: modern digital hearing aids with circuitry that selectively reduces the amplification of noise are costly, though still not perfect (Hamilton, 2013). Even so, many older adults could benefit from a hearing aid even if their difficulties are not completely resolved. But successful hearing aid users need training in how to adjust the hearing aid, and professionals who fit older adults with hearing aids should be ready to provide support until older adults are confident that their use is worthwhile. One further consideration is that even though modern hearing aids may modify the intensity of sound, they do not address difficulties with auditory processing at the central (brain) level (Wingfield, Tun, & McCoy, 2005). The impact of hearing loss on cognitive functioning remains to be more fully determined (Chien & Lin, 2012).

In sum, hearing loss remains largely untreated in the older adult population. Hearing aids can assist with communication if they are properly fitted and if older adults learn how to make the best use of them. But based on the statistics mentioned earlier, older adults do not seem eager to purchase them, and even when they do, they do not always use them. Even so, to assume that older adults are just stubborn is shortsighted and overly simplistic. The reasons older adults do not use hearing aids include denial of aging, the desire not to seem old and stupid, the expense, the difficulty of getting the devices to work just right, and negative experiences with older and less precise models. It is important to fully understand the reason(s) many older adults elect to miss out on the conversation rather than wear a hearing aid if we want to be effective educators regarding the potential value of these devices.

## You can't be too careful (or … falling down and crashing cars)

No one likes to fall down or crash a car. But older people, in their presumed frailty, seem most at risk. Is this because they actually fall and crash more than anyone else? Should we worry about our own older relatives whenever they go out on their own? What about making sure they get out from behind the driver's seat when they reach a certain age? The facts we examine in this section lead to the conclusion that the answer to each of these questions is a resounding *yes and no*. Older people do fall down. But maybe they don't worry about it as much as their younger relatives worry about it for them. As for problems behind the wheel, getting a driver for every Miss Daisy is not practical. Furthermore, it is not especially useful because older drivers don't crash cars all that much – it is safer to be on the road with them than it is to be on the road with certain other age groups. Maybe we should consider getting a driver for every Ferris Bueller instead.

## Older people worry too much about falling

Falls are a more serious concern for older adults than most people (including older adults themselves) actually realize. According to the Centers for Disease Control and Prevention (CDC, 2012), one out of every three adults over age 65 experiences a fall every year. Furthermore, plenty of folks fall more than once in a given year. In fact, falls are the leading cause of injury-related death in this age group. What about lasting consequences for those who do recover? Twenty to thirty percent of those who fall suffer moderate to severe injuries (e.g., hip fractures and head trauma), which can increase the risk of loss of independence and even early death. Although most otherwise healthy people who sustain these injuries are able to pick up their routines after treatment, those who had physical or cognitive problems before the injury may not be capable of returning to their former lifestyle.

Falls can happen anywhere, but well over half of them happen at home – during everyday activities (National Institute on Aging, National Institutes of Health, 2013). So staying home is not a good way to avoid falling. The floor might be wet, the rug might be loose, the nightlight might be out, and your shoes may be in the way. What if the bathroom does not have grab bars? If you lose your balance in the shower, you are going down!

The National Council on Aging (2013) sponsors a National Falls Prevention Awareness Day to convince older people not to think of falling as a normal part of aging. Some of the risk factors for falling include muscle weakness, balance or gait problems, blood pressure dropping when standing up, slow reflexes, foot problems, vision problems, confusion (even if it is brief), and medication side effects that lead to dizziness or confusion (and the more medications the greater the risk of that). When you think about it, most of these risks can be managed. People don't have to have weak muscles. They can exercise. They can use a cane or a walker if they have balance problems that can't be handled with medication. Many vision problems can be treated to some extent. Medication side effects can be monitored by a physician so that the person taking the medication does not have to fall down while taking it. Also, all of the things around the house that pose a danger can be improved.

Paradoxically, it turns out that fear of falling is itself a risk factor for falling. The fear can result in gait abnormalities and changes in postural control, both of which can increase the risk of falling (Delbaere, Crombez, Van Den Noortgate, Willems, & Cambier, 2006). Also, people who are afraid of falling down might limit their activities in order to avoid falls. This is a bad idea. Restricting activities can lead to physical decline (such as deconditioning, muscle atrophy, and poor balance) and could ultimately increase the risk of falls. Limiting activities might also result in limiting social contacts – this can lead to loneliness or depression (Scheffer, Schuurmans, van Dijk, van der Hooft, & de Rooij, 2008).

Despite the prevalence of falling, there is evidence that plenty of older people are not as worried as they should be. For example, Yardley, Donovan-Hall, Francis, and Todd (2006) held focus groups with 66 community-dwelling adults aged 61 to 94 in the U.K. to explore their perceptions of fall-prevention advice. These individuals tended to react positively to advice about the benefits of exercise for balance and mobility. However, their attitude was mixed when it came to lifestyle-related fall prevention suggestions. They explained that they had good reasons for the type of eyewear or footwear they used or for the furnishings in their homes, all of which carried some risk. For example, women who were 74, 78, and 88 years old and who had recently fallen rejected the idea of wearing padded hip protectors for reasons of vanity. A common response to the necessity for prevention advice was that it was important only for *other* people, typically people older than themselves. Some who had themselves recently fallen attributed the fall to a one-time lapse (e.g., inattention or illness). Some of the participants indicated that it was an issue of pride – getting a leaflet on fall prevention would imply that they are senile, ancient, or devoid of common sense.

In sum, if one in three of your peers fell down this year, why *shouldn't* you be worried? And not only that, but among some of your friends who have experienced a fall, life will not be the same ever again. Clearly, some older adults may worry about falling, but it is hard to say that they worry too much – the threat is real and should be taken more seriously by everyone. Of course, if fear limits older adults' enjoyment of life outside the home, it is too much fear – especially because the real threat is right there in the home! People do have to see to it that their homes are made as safe as possible. If a worry is based in reality, as is the fear of falling, then interventions (even at the family level) that aim to reduce the worry without reducing the risk are not ameliorating a problem that really can be helped. And let's not forget that only *some* older adults worry about falling. A significant number think that falling is someone else's problem.

# Older people get into more car accidents than younger people

In a study of older driver stereotypes, young adult participants described typical older drivers as unsafe and dangerous (Joanisse, Gagnon, & Voloaca, 2012). News reports about accidents caused by older drivers are certainly sensational. There was the incident in an open-air market in Santa Monica in 2003 in which an 86-year-old man stepped on the gas pedal instead of the brake pedal. Ten people were killed and 63 were injured. We also read about incidents in which older drivers crash through walls, like the 89-year-old woman on her way to a hair salon in Marlboro, Massachusetts, in 2012. She was aiming for a handicap parking space in front of a storefront office but instead went flying though the hedges and into the building. No one was hurt that time, but she missed a group of people by only a few inches. Reports like these contribute to the myth that older people are more prone than any other age group to get into accidents and that we need to get older folks off the road.

However, the drivers we should really be most afraid of are the 16- to 19-year-olds. They actually have the highest number of moving violations and crashes. According to the U.S. Census Bureau (2012), in 2009, people 19 years and younger made up 4.9% of the drivers but accounted for 12.2% of the accidents. By contrast, people 75 and older made up 6.5% of the drivers but accounted for only 3.3% of the accidents. It is true that older people drive fewer miles overall than do people in other age groups, but even by those calculations they are not as dangerous as teenagers.

According to the Centers for Disease Control and Prevention (CDC, 2013b), older adults are doing some things right. More than three-quarters of older drivers and passengers who were in fatal car crashes in 2009 were wearing seat belts – a higher proportion than in any other age group. Older drivers are also more likely to take to the road when conditions are the safest, avoiding nighttime and bad weather. Furthermore, they are less likely to be driving while impaired. For example, only 5% of older drivers involved in fatal crashes had a blood alcohol concentration higher than .08, compared with 25% of drivers between the ages of 21 and 64.

According to the Insurance Institute for Highway Safety (IIHS, 2014), between 1997 and 2012, fatal crash involvement for drivers aged 70 and older declined at a faster rate than did fatal crash involvement for drivers aged 35 to 54. Furthermore, these reductions were the greatest among the oldest drivers (80+). Also, based on insurance claims, the IIHS found that property damage claims start increasing after about age 65, but they never reach as high a level as the claims for the youngest drivers.

In a study of U.S. data on both fatal and non-fatal crashes, including data supplied by nine insurers, Braver and Trempel (2004) found that drivers aged 75 and older had actually killed fewer people outside of their own cars than did drivers aged 30 to 59. However, people inside their cars, including older drivers themselves, were not so lucky, perhaps because both they and their passengers tend to be frail. Non-fatal injury and property losses are a different story, however. Bodily injury liability claims nearly doubled for drivers aged 85 and older compared with those aged 30 to 59. Property damage liability claims were at their lowest for drivers aged 60 to 69 but increased dramatically after that, doubling for drivers 85 and older.

Let's get back to crashing into crowds at open-air markets and storefronts when drivers confuse the gas pedal with the brakes. What situations are really the most risky for older drivers? Intersections. Older drivers are much more likely than younger drivers to crash at intersections (Mayhew, Simpson, & Ferguson, 2006). Therefore, Braitman, Kirley, Chaudhary, and Ferguson (2007) studied the causes of intersection crashes among two groups of older drivers, those aged 70 to 79 and those aged 80 and older. Failure to yield the right of way was a problem that increased with age among older drivers, and it occurred mostly at stop signs, especially when drivers were trying to turn left. Admittedly, this is a complex situation, and it is particularly fraught for many of us. The researchers found that the drivers aged 70 to 79 made more evaluation errors such as seeing another car approaching but being wrong about how much time there was available to make the turn. Those 80 and over who crashed were more likely to have failed to notice the other car at all. Yikes! Thank goodness older drivers are not likely to be texting while driving.

As of June 2014, 29 states and the District of Columbia had implemented special requirements for people aged 65 or 70 and older who want to renew their drivers' licenses. These requirements vary, but include accelerated renewal cycles with shorter periods between renewals, requirements to renew in person rather than by mail or electronically, and testing that is over and above what is routinely required for younger drivers (e.g., road tests). If there is an issue about continued fitness for driving (e.g., a history of crashes, a report by a physician, or something noticed in the person's demeanor at renewal), states may require physical exams or a full retake of the standard licensing test – again, something not required for a typical renewal. Rather than refusing to renew a license altogether, a state might impose restrictions based on the outcome of the tests. Restrictions might include prohibition of nighttime driving, requiring additional mirrors on the vehicle, or limiting the distance from home that a person may drive (IIHS, 2014).

Unfortunately, the effectiveness of such special regulations for license renewal has not yet been established. The Insurance Institute for Highway Safety cites studies showing that vision testing for older adults is associated with lower fatal crash rates. According to the IIHS (2014), one study found that states with laws requiring in-person driver's license renewals had a 17% lower fatality rate per licensed driver among the oldest drivers (85+) compared with states without such laws. However, the IIHS notes that another study found that for drivers aged 65 and older, fatality rates per licensed driver did not differ between states with laws and states without laws for vision testing, road testing, or shortened renewal periods.

There is some self-limiting going on, however. An IIHS study (2014) of over 2,500 drivers aged 65 and older in three states showed that as people get older, they drive fewer miles. They avoid night driving, make fewer trips, travel shorter distances, and avoid driving on interstate highways and roads that are icy or snowy. Even people who know they have been diagnosed with mild Alzheimer's disease have been shown (through real-life in-car video recording) to confine their driving to daytime hours, sunny weather, light traffic, residential environments, and situations that involve no passengers. In this case, it is likely that although they had passed their state road test in order to be eligible to participate in the study, they regulated their driving behavior based on the knowledge of their diagnosis (Festa, Ott, Manning, Davis, & Heindel, 2012).

With regard to the effectiveness of driver education for older adults, Marottoli (2007) conducted a study for the AAA Foundation for Traffic Safety to assess the effectiveness of an education program that included classroom and road training. Participants were 126 drivers aged 70 and older. The experimental group had two four-hour classes and two one-hour on-road sessions that were focused on common problem areas for older drivers. The control group had a different course in vehicle, home, and environment safety that was presented to them individually. They had no on-road sessions. After the intervention, the experimental group did better than the control group on both written tests and road tests. The IIHS (2014) notes, however, that we should be cautious about taking findings like this at face value because drivers who take these courses tend to have lower crash rates even before taking the course than do those who opt not to take these courses. That makes the effectiveness of these courses difficult to evaluate.

Now let's consider the reasons older people may have reduced competency behind the wheel. One we have hinted at already: visual acuity. The type of vision required for driving is quite complex. Researchers have focused on *useful field of view* (UFOV) to identify vision requirements for driving that may capture the type of vision needed for driving more realistically than the typical acuity test. As reported in the *Monitor on Psychology* (DeAngelis, 2009, November), psychologist Karlene Ball developed the concept of UFOV while still a graduate student. As its name implies, UFOV is the spatial area that you can pay attention to in a glance – without head or eye movement. It varies depending on the task and it also varies across individuals. Obviously, acuity is part of it, but so is the ability to ignore distraction, to divide your attention, and to process what is going on in that visual space both quickly and effectively. Thus, in addition to pure visual acuity, UFOV includes some cognitive abilities. There is ample evidence that UFOV declines with age (e.g., Sekuler, Bennett, & Mamelak, 2000) and that it is associated with driving performance in older adults (Ball et al., 2005).

Ball initiated the development of a computerized UFOV test (Visual Awareness Research Group, Inc., 2009) that consists of three parts designed to assess visual processing under increasingly complex task demands. In the first part (processing speed), the examinee identifies a target that is presented briefly (an icon of either a car or a truck) in a box in the center of a screen. In the second part (divided attention), the examinee does the same thing, but this time must also indicate where on the periphery another target (always a car) appears simultaneously. In the third part (selective attention), the task is the same as in the second part, but the car on the periphery is embedded in a field of 47 triangles. "'We do all kinds of things to mess them up!'" quipped Ball (DeAngelis, 2009, November).

UFOV seems to be amenable to improvement with training. In one study (Roenker, Cissell, Ball, Wadley, & Edwards, 2003), older adults who received speed-of-processing training were tested 18 months later. They improved on their UFOV test and undertook fewer dangerous maneuvers in an open-road driving evaluation. Unfortunately, it is not yet standard practice for states to test UFOV as a requirement for obtaining a driver's license.

In addition to UFOV problems, older adults experience more difficulties with divided attention than do younger adults. In one study (McKnight & McKnight, 1993), young, middle-aged, and older adults viewed videos of traffic situations and responded to them using simulated vehicle controls. At the same time, some of them engaged in distracting activities such as talking on a cell phone. The oldest group (aged 50 to 80) was more likely than the other groups to make inappropriate responses on the simulated controls when distracted.

Additional factors may impair the ability of older drivers. For example, cataracts reduce contrast sensitivity by increasing glare. Reaction time slowing is a consequence of normal aging (Kausler, Kausler, & Krupshaw, 2007), and it is easy to see how reaction time could be a problem when drivers have to make a split-second decision about whether to step on the gas or the brake.

We've provided a few reasons why older adults might be at a disadvantage when driving. At the same time, we should recognize the wide variability among older adults with regard to reaction time and attentional capabilities. Also, many older adults recognize their limitations. As we have noted, they self-limit and drive only when they consider it likely that they will not have difficulties. Also, some older adults know that it can be risky to carry on conversations while driving – they recognize they must focus all their attention on the road when traveling to their destination. We know of one older driver who refuses to drive with a passenger because she realizes that she is safest if she is not distracted with conversation.

Giving up a driver's license is fraught with issues of independence for older adults. This is not surprising, given that (with a few exceptions in urban areas such as New York City) public transportation is not an adequate substitute for being able to drive one's own car. It would be reasonable, however, to initiate changes in the driving environment. More left-turn lanes and traffic light arrows would mitigate the dangers at intersections. So would replacing stop signs with traffic lights. Obviously, there is room for improvement by making signs more visible and by posting warning signs well in advance of danger areas. Making improvements in automobiles themselves is more problematic. If we add extra information to the dashboard that might help younger drivers, older drivers may be overloaded with too many things to pay attention to. However, devices could be installed to enhance environmental warnings. An extra sound coming from the car would be useful for someone who cannot hear the ambulance siren soon enough to pull over.

In conclusion, where do we stand on the myth that older people get into more accidents than younger people? They are emphatically safer than the youngest drivers. They are cautious about when and where they drive, they wear seatbelts, and they don't drink and drive as much as do younger people. True, age-related perceptual and cognitive difficulties can impair driving. Older people tend to be aware of these problems, but we can do better as a society to make the roads safer for them and thus for all of us. There is a lot of room for creativity in this endeavor, and understanding the needs of older people in this regard is the place to start.

## Now that you don't have sex anymore...

Do older people lose interest in sex or do younger people resist the idea that they don't? Talking about older people's sexuality is a sure-fire way to find out where ageism is lurking in our society. According to the Pew Research Center (2009), for many people, losing interest in sex is literally a defining feature of old age: 46% of the 18- to 29-year-olds surveyed agreed with the notion that a person is old when he or she is no longer sexually active. In the sections that follow we will try to convince you that most grandparents and many great-grandparents are still feeling sexy and want to be attractive to potential partners. It is not really nice for people to assume otherwise; in fact, it is demeaning. Advertisers have learned that it pays to treat the situation with more respect. Grownups with bladder problems are not likely to buy products called *diapers*, so it seems only reasonable for everyone else to treat the medical problem of incontinence with more dignity. Nevertheless, 51% of adults aged 18 to 29 surveyed by the Pew Research Center (2009) endorsed the opinion that bladder-control problems are a marker for old age. Finally, let's accept the fact that some people are doing just fine by themselves. Not every older person needs to be married to be happy or to be safe.

## Myth #5 Older people lose interest in sex

There is a great deal of research on the importance that people place on their sexuality across the lifespan. In general, there is no evidence that older people lose interest in sex. According to the National Social Life, Health and Aging Project (Waite, Laumann, Das, & Schumm, 2009), 73.6% of women and 71.7% of men aged 75 to 85 said that satisfactory sex is essential to maintaining a relationship. Even more telling is an AARP/*Modern Maturity* survey (AARP, 1999) of 1,384 adults aged 45 and older (average age was 60 for men and 61 for women), which found that only 1.9% of the men and 4.9% of the women agreed that sex is only for younger people.

Here's how 93-year-old Roger Angell, long-time editor at the *New Yorker*, speaks of the need for intimacy after the death of his wife:

> Getting old is the second-biggest surprise of my life, but the first, by a mile, is our increasing need for deep attachment and intimate love. We oldies yearn daily and hourly for conversation and a renewed domesticity ... for someone close by in the car when coming home at night ... This is why we

throng Match.com and OkCupid in such numbers – but not just for this ... everyone in the world wants to be with someone else tonight, together in the dark, with the sweet warmth of a hip or a foot or a bare expanse of shoulder within reach. (2014, February 17 & 24, p. 65)

Apparently, sex is important to the majority of older adults, but how is this fact reflected in their behavior? In a study of 2,783 Australian men aged 70 to 95 (Hyde et al., 2010), one-third reported that they were sexually active. In a U.S. study using data from a nationally representative sample of 3,005 adults who participated in the National Social Life, Health, and Aging Project, 72% of the men and 45.5% of the women aged 57 to 72 reported that they were sexually active (Karraker, DeLamater, & Schwartz, 2011). Waite et al. (2009) found that for those heterosexual men and women aged 75 to 84 (in the same National Social Life, Health, and Aging Project sample) who did report being sexually active, the rates of sexual activity remained constant from age 65 to 75 with only a small decline after that. As for the type of sexual activity in which they engaged, 87% of women and 91% of men between the ages of 57 and 84 said that vaginal sex was always or usually part of their sexual activity. Individuals between the ages of 75 and 85 reported somewhat less frequent vaginal intercourse, but no decrease at all in hugging, kissing, or other sexual touching.

Despite the desire for a full sexual life, there can be barriers to sexual activity in the older age group. For heterosexual women, the lack of an available partner is a serious problem. Starting at age 40, there are more women than men in the population, and by age 85 the ratio is about 2 to 1 (Karraker et al., 2011). Add to that the fact that older men tend to choose younger women when they become widowed or divorced, and the pool of available men for older women is even more diminished. Susan Sontag (1972, September 23) put this dilemma in emotional terms: "Thus, for most women, aging means a humiliating process of gradual sexual disqualification" (p. 32).

The disproportionate sex ratio also means that older men are more likely than older women to be married – 72% of men aged 65 and older are married but only 45% of women aged 65 and older are married (U.S. Department of Health and Human Services, Administration on Aging, Administration for Community Living, 2012). According to Karraker et al. (2011), a change in marital status is unrelated to any decline in sexual activity for men aged 57 to 85. Among women in that age range, however, the change from married to widowed explains a good part of any decline in sexual activity. In a survey of a nationally representative sample of people aged 57 to 85, Lindau et al. (2007) found that of those who were not in a marital or other intimate relationship, 22% of men and 4% of women reported they had been sexually active in the previous year. Clearly, the lack of an available partner interferes with sexual frequency for women more than it does for men.

When people answer surveys about their interest in sex, they may be influenced by their own life situation. That is, it's possible to imagine people saying they are not interested in having sex if there is nobody available for them to have sex with. Even so, they may still feel sexy, so perhaps they masturbate. DeLamater (2012) looked at data on masturbation from the National Survey of Sexual Health and Behavior conducted in 2009. It turns out that adults aged 70 and older engage in a fair amount of masturbation: 46% of men and 33% of women reported engaging in solo masturbation. However, there does seem to be a decline with age: 72% of men and 54% of women in their 50s reported that they masturbated alone.

Does decline in physical health explain some of the decline in sexual activity? Yes, it does, and some studies (e.g., Karraker et al., 2011) indicate that this is especially true for men. Lindau et al. (2007) found that in a sample of over 3,000 men and women aged 57 to 85 who were in an intimate relationship but had been sexually inactive for three months or more, the most common reason for sexual inactivity was the male partner's physical health. Any decline in a husband's health is bound to affect the frequency of partnered sexual activity for the wife as well. A study conducted by the AARP in 2010 shows a strong relationship between a positive rating of one's health and reported frequency of sexual intercourse. In another AARP survey (1999), among the oldest respondents (aged 75 and older), only 45% of men and 13% of women said they had any condition that restricted sexual activity. Once again, note that men's physical health status is probably more responsible for any decline in sexual activity for older couples. Finally, what about those sexual problems we hear so much about – erectile dysfunction, menopausal issues, and so on? Of respondents to the 2010 AARP survey, 29% of men and 13% of women responded "yes" when asked if they had ever had problems with sexual functioning. The percentage reporting problems increased with age for men (23% for those aged 45 to 49 and 38% for those aged 70 and older), but there was no increase for women.

Let's look at erectile dysfunction (ED) first. Shabsigh (2006) reminds us that back in 1948, Kinsey found that the prevalence of ED increased with age from 0.1% at age 20 to 75% at age 80. These percentages of ED by age still seem to apply today. A study conducted by the Harvard School of Public Health (Bacon et al., 2003) on more than 31,000 men aged 53 to 90 also indicates that, sure enough, not much has changed: fewer than 2% of the men in the study who reported that they had erection problems experienced them before age 40. The increase in the percentage who experienced problems was steady thereafter: 4% between ages 40 and 49, 26% between 50 and 59, 40% between 60 and 69, and 71% for men aged 70 and over. The good news is that the men in that study who were physically active, didn't smoke, drank alcohol only moderately, and generally kept their cardiovascular system healthy (an erection is a vascular phenomenon, after all) had a 30% lower risk than the rest. And don't forget, there is treatment today for ED that wasn't around in Kinsey's era: Viagra®, Cialis®, Levitra®, and others. As of 1999, about 10% of men reported that they had used medications or hormones to improve sexual function (AARP, 1999).

Television commercials for Viagra and Cialis have made ED easier to discuss among the general population. However, changes in women's physiology with age haven't gotten as much (positive) screen time. For older women, postmenopausal vaginal changes are a concern. With menopause, levels of estrogen decline, and this causes the tissue lining the inside of the vagina to become thin. In turn, this causes other cell and tissue changes that result in decreased vaginal blood flow and vaginal lubrication. In addition, pH changes cause certain bacteria to proliferate, which in turn can cause infection and inflammation that can make intercourse painful. MacBride, Rhodes, and Shuster's (2010) review of studies on this topic indicated that the prevalence of these symptoms is about 4% in early premenopausal women, but it increases to 47% in late postmenopausal women. They also note that breast cancer survivors – over 2.8 million women in the U.S. as of September, 2013 (American Cancer Society, 2013) – have a higher rate of vaginal symptoms because treatments for breast cancer can affect hormone levels.

Thus, it is possible that nearly half of older women suffer pain during intercourse due to lack of lubrication, frequent urinary tract infections, small tears in the vaginal tissue, and so on. Low-dose vaginal estrogen cream may be a good solution for many of them. Over-the-counter long-acting moisturizers like Replens® can be effective. And of course there are lots of lubricants for use during sex – and we do see those products beginning to appear in TV ads. Unfortunately, current cohorts of older women are a bit shy about reporting pain during intercourse to their physicians. Furthermore, they may have bought into the very myth that we are discussing: sex is for the young. Therefore, they do not seek treatment and we do not have accurate statistics about prevalence. But perhaps the cohort of women who are in their 50s and early 60s today came of age at a time when it was less difficult to discuss sex, and they may report problems to their physicians with greater alacrity.

One thing for sure is that the "ick" factor, which is part of the current culture on issues of older adult sexuality, is one of the more blatant forms of ageism in today's society. Young adults do not want to think about their grandparents having sex with each other or masturbating when they are thought to be reading alone in their beds. Advertisements for ED drugs play into this stereotype by featuring men who appear to be middle-aged – men who look fit and are just beginning to gray but are feeling sexy about their stylish, 40ish female companions. There is no 75-year-old in the picture. The same goes for ads for vaginal lubricants (oops, the products are called *personal lubricants*, perhaps because people don't want to ask a salesperson for help finding a product with *vagina* in its name).

But get ready for some edgy new advertising. Late in 2012, Canadian ads for Mae by Damiva® (think dame, diva, and Mae West – remembered for her raunchy sexuality in films of the 1930s and 1940s) look like this: "Get ready to feel like a teenager again, but with better judgment. Hi, I'm Mae and I naturally restore vaginal moisture. Your vagina, and your honey, will thank you" (Cullers, 2012, November 28).

Another way that ageism about sexuality can play out is in the infantilizing of the romantic side of older adult relationships. "Aren't they cute?" is a way of desexualizing an affectionate older couple. When people think this way, they are able to look at an older couple (who are, for example, holding hands in public) and not have to think about what they do in bed – it's as if a pair of 4-year-olds were holding hands.

The fact that our culture desexualizes older adults can ultimately present problems for them. They may be less informed about how to protect themselves from and monitor themselves for STDs. However, STDs can be a problem even in late adulthood. It's also easy to imagine that when older adults go through a course of rehabilitation (e.g., after a broken hip), there are sex positions that would be safe and comfortable for them, but it is unlikely that this issue is covered in every rehabilitation environment. Also, as DeLamater (2012) suggests, some older people are under the mistaken impression that they should not have sex if they or their partners have had major health problems, such as heart attacks. If they don't obtain adequate sex education from medical personnel, they may buy into the stereotype that they should not be interested in sex anymore.

Many people find it disturbing that even people with dementia who reside in nursing homes may seek sexual intimacy. Bryan Gruley at

Bloomberg.com (2013, July 22) recently reported on a case from an Iowa nursing home. A 78-year-old man was found having intercourse with an 87-year-old woman. Both had dementia. The question for the nursing home administrators was whether these residents had the capacity to consent. Federal and state laws require that nursing homes respect residents' right to privacy but also guarantee their safety. This requirement is enforced very differently in different locations. In the Iowa case, the authorities decided that both residents were calmer and happier together than apart. However, the woman's family filed a lawsuit against the nursing home, claiming that she had been raped. Yet Gruley cites experts who argue that even when people are too cognitively impaired to make financial decisions, they are able to decide whether they want to have sex at any given moment.

Bottom line: It is a myth that all older people lose interest in sex, though some may. There are health problems, both general and sexual, that do increase with age, but the majority of people can be treated for them. Nevertheless, one thing is certain: Young people do not like to think that older people (especially their parents and grandparents!) are having sex or even thinking about it, as dramatized by this interchange between Homer Simpson and Grampa Simpson:

GRAMPA: "Welcome home, Son. I broke two lamps and lost all your mail. What's wrong with your wife?"
HOMER: "Never mind, you wouldn't understand."
GRAMPA: "Flu?"
HOMER: "No."
GRAMPA: "Protein deficiency?"
HOMER: "No."
GRAMPA: "Pneumonoultramicroscopicsilicovolcanoconiosis?"
HOMER: "No."
GRAMPA: "Unsatisfying sex life?"
HOMER: "N– yes! But please, don't you say that word!"
GRAMPA: "What, seeeex? What's so unappealing about hearing your elderly father talk about sex? I had sex."

## Older women do not care about their looks

Look at the birthday cards in the "humor" section of your local card shop. Such cards exemplify the cultural stereotype that older women tend to be saggy, baggy, and dowdy. Greeting cards certainly do their share to perpetuate a myth that older women are unattractive and have no interest whatsoever in looking physically appealing and chic.

In her classic essay, Sontag (1972, September 23) observed that in American culture, there is a *double standard of aging* – we view signs of aging more negatively in women than in men.

> Only one standard of female beauty is sanctioned: the *girl*. The great advantage men have is that our culture allows two standards of male beauty: the *boy* and the *man* ... A man does not grieve when he loses the smooth, unlined, hairless skin of a boy. For he has only exchanged one form of attractiveness for another ... There is no equivalent of this second standard for women ... Every wrinkle, every line, every grey hair is a defeat ... the standard of beauty in a woman of any age is how far she retains, or how she manages to simulate, the appearance of youth.(p. 36)

Of 3,200 women aged 18 to 64 who participated in a global study by Etcoff, Orbach, Scott, and D'Agostino (2004), only 2% considered themselves to be beautiful. A larger proportion of these women were more comfortable calling themselves *natural* (31%) or *average* (29%). Many of the women, especially those who were more satisfied with their own appearance, thought that non-physical factors (e.g., happiness, confidence, dignity, humor, and intelligence) contribute to making a woman beautiful. Those who were less satisfied with their appearance were more likely to think that cosmetics make a woman beautiful. Nevertheless, 89% of the respondents strongly agreed that "A woman can be beautiful at any age" (p. 40). At the same time, 75% of the women strongly agreed that they wished "the media did a better job of portraying women of diverse physical attractiveness – age, shape and size" (p. 43). The older women in this study (aged 45 to 64) expressed a clear interest in seeing attractive women of different ages depicted in the media.

Some women are bound to respond to ageism by minimizing visible signs of their own aging as much as possible (including everything from hair dye to cosmetic surgery). This behavior is sometimes referred to as *beauty work*. Hurd Clarke and Griffin (2008) interviewed 44 women aged 50 to 70 about beauty work. More than half of the women admitted to using hair dyes, and 37 out of the 44 said they used make-up. A small number (6 or fewer) reported that they had had surgical procedures (e.g., liposuction) or non-surgical cosmetic procedures (e.g., chemical peels, Botox®).

Cosmetic procedures have become more popular every year. The American Society for Aesthetic Plastic Surgery (2012) reported that in the years 1997 to 2012 there was an 80% increase in the number of cosmetic surgical procedures performed and a nearly 500% increase in the number of minimally invasive procedures (e.g., skin resurfacing). If older women do not care about their looks, how can we explain the fact that, in 2012, 30% of surgical procedures and 38% of nonsurgical procedures performed were on people over the age of 50? Eyelid surgery (85% were women), facelifts (90% were women), and liposuction (87% were women) were the most popular surgeries in that age group, whereas breast augmentation and nose jobs were more popular with younger adults. Some of the women in the Hurd Clarke and Griffin (2008) study who had had beauty work done gave reasons related to their attempts to feel less invisible to potential sexual partners. Another reason for beauty work was to avoid feeling discriminated against in the workplace. In general, these women acknowledged that the societal emphasis on youthful appearance affected their self-esteem.

How do we feel about others who do beauty work? Harvard Medical School researcher Nancy Etcoff, quoted in the *New York Times* (Ellin, 2011, August 8), is supportive of women who want to have procedures that make them look younger: "'If an older woman wants to regain eyelids or wants a breast that she doesn't have to tuck into a waistband, then why not?'" Etcoff contends that our culture offers mixed messages about older people who actively look for romance. "'Here we are in the age of Viagra, which is very well accepted, but suddenly the idea of older people, mostly women, wanting to be sexually attractive at that age makes us uncomfortable.'"

Harris (1994) investigated how people judge others who use cosmetic procedures such as hair dye, facelifts, and wrinkle cream. Participants (men and women aged 18 to 80) read a scenario about a man or a woman who was described as having gray hair, sagging skin, and wrinkles. Half of the participants were told that the man or woman in the scenario used age-concealment techniques. As we might expect, respondents thought that most of those physical signs of aging were unattractive. Even so, they did not have a favorable view of those who used age-concealment techniques, although they found it somewhat more acceptable for women than they did for men. Ironically, however, respondents (both male and female) found it perfectly acceptable to use these techniques on themselves. Go figure.

In the years since Sontag wrote her 1972 essay on the double standard of aging, evolutionary psychologists have weighed in on why the double standard might exist. In a classic study, Buss (1989) argued that men value physical attractiveness and youth in women because they see it as a cue of health and thus high reproductive capacity. By contrast, in all 37 of the cultures that Buss studied, women preferred somewhat older men.

He contends that older men are desirable because their mature age provides cues for longevity, maturity, prowess, and experience – all cues that they will be good providers. Buss reminds us that this preference seems to exist even among nonhuman species. This theory has not been without controversy, but there has not been much disagreement about the fact that older men seem to make acceptable mates for younger women, but most often not the other way around.

What about gay men and lesbians? This gets complicated, and the prediction here is not as straightforward. Silverthorne and Quinsey (2000) asked 18- to 52-year-olds to look at facial pictures of people of different ages and rate how sexually attractive they found each face to be. Regardless of their sexual orientation, men showed a preference for the younger faces of their preferred sex. For both straight women and lesbians it was the reverse – regardless of their sexual orientation they preferred the older faces of their preferred sex. Thus, regardless of sexual orientation, the double standard holds up: men want younger partners and women want older partners.

However, in a study that included both straight and gay men and women aged 16 to 83 (Teuscher & Teuscher, 2007), everyone rated the younger-looking faces they were shown as more attractive than the older-looking faces – and this was the case for both male and female raters regardless of their sexual orientation. Nevertheless, if they were told that the face was a potential sexual partner (i.e., a man's face for a straight woman or a gay man and a woman's face for a straight man or a lesbian), the men's preference for youth was more pronounced than the women's preference.

Given the stigma of physical aging, the recent trend to emphasize stylish aging is especially interesting. Take a look at Ari Seth Cohen's blog (http://advancedstyle.blogspot.com/) or book (*Advanced Style*) for some images of fabulous women over 60. The over-50 crowd now includes celebrities such as Holly Hunter, Michelle Pfeiffer, Sharon Stone, Melanie Griffith, and Madonna. Www.askmen.com names the top 10 sexiest ladies over 60: Meryl Streep (b. 1949), Helen Mirren (b. 1945), Susan Sarandon (b. 1946), Lauren Hutton (b. 1943), and Tina Turner (b. 1939) are on the list.

In a *New York Times* feature, Mireille Silcoff (2013, April 26) speculates on a phenomenon she calls *Eldertopia*, which is a "pro-aged paradise lovingly promoted by people who are themselves not even close to middle-aged." She claims that the interest in "cool old people" is a way of saying, "'This is how I want to be when I get old.'" This view may explain how a 2010 Facebook petition got actress Betty White (b. 1922) to host *Saturday Night Live*. Silcoff thinks the driving force for the trend toward Eldertopia is related to the stress the younger generation feels about having to live up to cultural norms. They would like to think that they can age into a feeling of being immune to that pressure – they can stop worrying about looking hot or being cool, and instead, achieve this "chosen aesthetic – this doddering chic ... the imagined authenticity of old age."

In addition to the possibility of a stylish older age, there seems to be a gradual cultural shift, which values a look that implies vital middle age. Dr. Macrena Alexiades-Armenakas is a dermatologist with a Park Avenue practice who was profiled in a *New York Times* feature (Schwartz, 2013, July 31). She has developed a highly successful practice that includes New York professional women concerned about being perceived as too old. However, they are not looking for a youthful image. Rather, they are "aiming for a cosmetic sweet spot: old enough to command respect, yet fresh enough to remain vital ... eternal early middle age."

In summary, it seems that older women do indeed care about their looks. They are fully aware of the double standard of aging and they know that reducing signs of physical aging is in their best interest. It should not be surprising that women have most of the cosmetic procedures. Fortunately, we are entering a period that may be getting friendlier to older women, as evidenced by the recent hype about chic older women who maintain their style without disguising their age.

## Myth 7 Older people need to wear diapers, and how sexy is that?

There is a myth that as people grow older, they are bound to have serious issues with bladder control and, inevitably, they will experience sufficient leakage to necessitate the need for diapers. Let's start with an explanation of the medical issues that could result in leakage. Urinary incontinence (UI) is the loss of bladder control (the National Institutes of Health website is a good source for information about this topic: http://www.nlm.nih.gov/medlineplus/urinaryincontinence.html#cat1).

UI actually includes everything from a little leak to a complete wetting. If it occurs because bladder muscles are weak, then it is the sort of leaking that occurs with sneezing or having a giggle fit. That is called *stress incontinence*, which is the most common type of UI and is usually a problem for women more than for men. Stress incontinence can affect even young and middle-aged women. In fact, childbirth can weaken those muscles.

If bladder muscles are too active, the reverse can happen – you feel you have to go but you really only have a bit of urine in your bladder. That is called *urge incontinence*. This sort of UI can increase with age. Urge incontinence is a problem because even though you don't have much urine to pass, you may not make it in time to the bathroom. Urge incontinence can occur with diabetes, Alzheimer's disease, Parkinson's disease, multiple sclerosis, and stroke.

Another type of UI, *overflow incontinence*, can happen when a little bit of urine leaks from a bladder that always seems full. This is often a male problem and can be caused by an enlarged prostate. Finally, *functional incontinence* occurs when you can't make it to the bathroom because of some unrelated problem such as arthritis, which makes it hard to move quickly.

How prevalent is UI? In a large study that sampled people with AARP Medicare supplement insurance (Hawkins et al., 2011), 37.5% of the respondents reported having some type of urinary incontinence. In addition to advancing age, the strongest predictors were being female and being obese. For the people in this study, the negative effect of UI on quality of life (both physical and social well-being) was even greater than that experienced with problems such as diabetes, cancer, and arthritis. Yet, only 59.4% of the respondents said they had spoken to their doctor about it. This fact is surprising, especially in light of a study by Sims, Browning, Lundgren-Lindquist, and Kendig (2011), which found that mood was negatively affected even when individuals had only low levels of urge incontinence.

Fortunately, there is help for many older adults who do have UI. Pelvic muscle exercises (*Kegel exercises*) are prescribed to strengthen the muscle that helps you hold it in. Holding it in is an important skill that is taken for granted by those who can do it. Another treatment sometimes recommended is called *timed voiding*, which involves urinating on a schedule.

In some cases, lifestyle changes are called for: losing weight, giving up smoking, cutting down on alcohol and caffeine. In some cases medications can be prescribed, depending on the cause of the problem. For example, estrogen cream is sometimes helpful for older women with mild stress incontinence. Surgery may be an option if UI is due to the position of the bladder or to an enlarged prostate.

Not only can UI be treated, but in many cases it can be prevented (Sievert et al., 2012). By middle age, women can begin to work on strengthening their pelvic floor muscles as part of an exercise routine. With lifestyle changes in at-risk populations such as those with obesity and diabetes (which can affect bladder functioning), UI can often be prevented. Providing information about the risk of incontinence to such people can be a motivator. What about the risk factor of childbirth? Pelvic floor muscle training may help those women too.

Now that we've gone over some facts on incontinence, let's move on to hygiene products that are designed for those who experience UI but have not been able to treat the problem with other means. Used effectively, such products can have a positive impact on the quality of life and can reduce any feelings of self-consciousness in those with UI. Unfortunately, such products are sometimes referred to as *adult diapers*. We noted in the myth "Older people lose interest in sex" our objection to infantilizing older adult sexuality ("Aren't they cute") as a way of desexualizing older adults for the comfort of younger adults. So what does it mean when we refer to urinary incontinence products as diapers? We don't refer to hygiene products related to menstruation as diapers. Interestingly, manufacturers are beginning to realize that they will be more effective in marketing such products to the large baby boomer generation if they respect these individuals and take care not to patronize them. To wit, these products are rarely referred to as diapers anymore. For example, Depend® (one of the major suppliers) advertises hygiene products as underwear and briefs, not diapers. And this company is beginning to court men in a specific advertising campaign (Neff, 2013, April 22):

> Former National Football League defensive tackle Tony Siragusa is telling men to put on pads – and it has nothing to do with football … It's the first time the Kimberly-Clark Corp. brand has used media advertising to highlight light bladder leakage for men, something the company says afflicts 23 million – including one in five men over 60 – a phenomenon far less discussed publicly than the same problem for women … Only 20% of men who suffer light bladder leakage use any products for it at all, and many who do so use women's products, [the Deputy Brand Director] said. The rest rely on makeshift solutions such as wadded up paper towels and toilet paper – or simply nothing and change their clothes as needed. Depend has had the Guards product on the market for years, but without specific media support, and is launching the smaller Shields as part of the new campaign. Both products have been designed or redesigned "to be more masculine."

In summary, UI is not inevitable in older adulthood. It can be a problem for about one-third of older adults at some time, but in many cases there are ways to treat it effectively. However, if people are shy about reporting it to their physician they are unlikely to get the help they need. Yet it is extremely important that they do so, because UI can have a negative impact on quality of life. It seems obvious that it would be beneficial for people to view UI as just another medical problem that needs diagnosis, treatment, and management. If the problem had less stigma associated with it, we would undoubtedly see a reduction in the negative psychological impact UI has on the people who experience it, and we would also see more people being proactive in managing the symptoms.

## Myth #8  It's always best for older adults to be married rather than single

As of 2012, 72% of men and 45% of women aged 65 and older were married (U.S. Department of Health and Human Services, Administration on Aging, Administration for Community Living, 2012). Are those married folks better off than the rest? The rest add up to an awful lot of people, after all. Are all of those married folks healthier, happier, less lonely, less depressed, and more satisfied with their lives than their unmarried counterparts?

Before we attempt to answer this question, we should note that *married* is not the only way to think of *not single*. We are fully aware that lots of people who are living in long-term committed relationships are not officially married. However, the research we rely on when we discuss this myth has been undertaken with married people as participants. Even so, we can certainly think more inclusively about this group. So when we use the term *married* in the discussion that follows, it is likely that what we say applies to couples who live as if married but who, for one reason or another, do not have a marriage license.

Clearly, being married has its advantages, so claiming that it's always best for older adults to be married does not seem like much of a myth. It goes without saying that combined households are more efficient economically than single ones. Also, as couples segue into their later years, it sometimes happens that one partner develops health issues that limit what he or she can do. Usually the other partner does not have the identical difficulties or limitations. This means that one member of an older couple may need help with something that the other member is capable of providing. In one instance we know of, the wife has such severe arthritis that she cannot drive herself to her frequent medical appointments or to the grocery store. In fact, there are very few days when she is well enough to navigate a grocery store even if someone drives her there. Fortunately, her husband is a capable driver, and he is certainly able to purchase whatever groceries the couple needs. Despite her disabilities, the wife is still capable of cooking and enjoys it, which is a good thing because the husband has no skills in the kitchen.

According to the U.S. Department of Health and Human Services, Administration on Aging, Administration for Community Living (2012), women make up more than two-thirds of the nursing home population. Why do we see nursing homes and assisted living facilities more populated by older women than by older men? A likely reason is that women tend to marry men of the same age or older. This, combined with women's longer life expectancy, means that women are more likely than men to be widowed and left living on their own and unable to manage in their later years. Living with a partner might have been a way to age more comfortably at home.

Given all we have reviewed, how can the statement, "It's always best for older adults to be married rather than single" be a myth? Well, simply because it is becoming more apparent in recent years that marriage may not be for everyone. This was illustrated pointedly in a classic study by Tucker, Wingard, Friedman, and Schwartz (1996), who examined data from 1,077 men and women who participated in the Terman Life-Cycle Longitudinal Study that was initiated in 1921. Terman's study participants were a select group of intelligent, educated, middle-class, primarily European American children born in 1910. Tucker et al. categorized the Terman study participants according to their marital status as of midlife (in 1950) as follows: (1) consistently married (married with no prior marital breakups); (2) inconsistently married (married, but with a prior marital breakup); (3) separated or divorced; (4) single. When the mortality of these individuals was checked in 1991, those who were married as of 1950 had lived longer than those separated or divorced as of 1950. So at first blush, it does appear that being married is preferable. However, several additional findings remind us that we should not jump to conclusions. First, in this select sample of educationally and economically privileged individuals, those who were single as of midlife (1950) had no greater mortality risk than those married as of 1950. Second, particularly for men, those who were married at midlife but had already experienced a marital breakup (inconsistently married) had a higher mortality risk than those who were consistently married. Tucker et al. speculated that marital breakup may have long-term negative effects that are not completely reduced by remarriage. Or perhaps marital inconsistency is associated with lower conscientiousness about health. In any case, Tucker el al.'s findings indicate that we should exercise caution before assuming marriage is a uniformly protective factor when it comes to longevity.

People often assume that couples married for decades are happy, satisfied, and in agreement on most issues. Carstensen, Gottman, and Levenson (1995) and Levenson, Carstensen, and Gottman (1993) studied middle-aged couples (aged 40–50 and married at least 15 years) and older couples (aged 60–70 and married at least 35 years). These couples, most in first marriages, lived in Berkeley, California, and were predominantly European American, upper-middle-class, and well-educated. The good news is that, overall, older couples reported fewer disagreements than middle-aged couples. Even so, there was considerable variation in study participants' responses to a self-report questionnaire on marital satisfaction. Those lower in satisfaction reported more disagreements than those higher in satisfaction. And among couples who were less satisfied, wives reported more physical and psychological symptoms than husbands did. It seems that as a group, men may be better off when married, but women are better off only when *happily* married. When the relationship is not fulfilling, women suffer more (physically and emotionally), whereas men tend to buffer themselves against health problems by withdrawing from conflict (Levenson et al., 1993).

In addition to collecting self-report data on marital satisfaction, Carstensen et al. (1995) made video recordings as each couple interacted during the course of a 15-minute conversation about a problem that they claimed was causing continuing disagreement in their marriage. Objective observers rated the emotional affect shown by members of the pair with regard to verbal content, voice tone, facial expression, gestures, and body movement. Compared with the middle-aged couples, the older couples displayed less emotion, both positive (interest, humor, joy) and negative (anger, disgust, belligerence, defensiveness, whining). However, in both middle-aged and older couples there were gender differences: the wives' facial expressions and verbal interactions showed more emotion, both positive and negative. In contrast, the husbands' facial expressions were more neutral and their verbal expression of emotion was more restrained. Husbands in the dissatisfied couples were especially avoidant of conflict.

Overall, these findings illustrate that even after many years of marriage, some couples are happy and satisfied, but others are not. Even in long-term marriages there can be dissatisfaction and negative emotions, though older couples may show more restraint in expressing them. In general, however, women seem to be more negatively affected by disharmony. Men may be better able to weather difficulties in a marital relationship.

When we refer to older adults who are not married, we must remember that they can be single for several reasons. Some older adults have always been single (never married), a category that is likely to become more common than it was in earlier decades. According to the CDC (2013a) the marriage rate in the U.S. has declined from 8.2 per 1,000 to 6.8 per 1,000 just in the first decade of the 21st century. DePaulo and Morris (2006) contend that despite the negative stereotypes associated with being single – the term they use is *singlism* – their review of research findings indicates that those who have always been single do not differ much in health and happiness compared with those who have been continuously married.

Some older adults are single because, once married, they are now divorced. Divorce can wreak economic havoc, especially if a marriage was long-term and particularly if one member of the pair (usually the woman) did not have a steady work career. Divorce can also be traumatic if one member of the pair was somehow in the dark that the marriage was not going so well. Even so, divorce can be preferable to an unhappy and unsatisfying marriage. In fact, movies have themes along these lines (e.g., *Eat Pray Love*).

Overall, the divorce rate in the U.S. is steady or declining. However, the divorce rate among middle-aged and older adults has doubled in the last two decades. So assuming that single older people are widowed is no longer accurate. In fact, one in four of the people who divorced in 2010 was 50 or older. Brown and Lin (2012) have studied what they call "the gray divorce revolution." In reporting on this phenomenon for the *New York Times*, Rachel Swarns (2012, March 1) noted that in 2010 about one-third of adults aged 46 to 64 were divorced, separated, or never married. This figure compares with only 13% in 1970. Many older single people have financial independence and prefer to keep it that way. But even if divorce results in financial instability, it can make some individuals feel liberated – especially after a period of living alone and coming to a point of feeling empowered by the independence. Swarns discussed the case of a divorced 55-year-old woman who has no health insurance or pension. She knows that the years ahead may hold economic hardship. Yet, she "still savors her freedom."

Finally, older adults can be single because their spouses have died. We tend to assume that older adults who are widowed want to remarry (we discuss a variation of this idea in Myth #34, "If older widows date, it's to find a new husband"). For our present purposes, let's discuss not just dating, but rather actual remarriage.

It is commonly believed that men who are widowed are better off if they remarry. Many people think men need a spouse to take charge of nutritional habits and to organize the couple's social life. If this is indeed the case, then men who are married or remarried are better off compared with men who are single. Also, as we noted earlier, married men seem less likely than married women to react to conflict.

But what about women? Are they always better off married? In a recent article in the *AARP Magazine*, Marion Winik (2013, August–September) describes her own experience with marriage and singlehood. She had two marriages, both of which she claimed had some positive and some negative qualities. Her first husband died young after a long illness. The second marriage started out well but deteriorated, so the reader assumes it ended in divorce. Subsequently, Winik describes how she spent a great deal of time and effort following the end of her second marriage seeking out a third marital partner. However, she suddenly realized she was happier single than she had ever been when married. After publishing a book on single living, she began seeing a man who lived an hour away. She reports that she cares for him and enjoys his company, but she likes the one-hour distance between them and has no intention of becoming a wife again. Rather, she is enjoying a rich life in singlehood with work and her relationships with adult children and friends. In her article, Winik mentions several researchers who have reported that people, especially older adults, are often content with singlehood.

In sum, there is no clear answer to the question of whether it is better for older people to be married. It depends. Financially, it's probably better to be married. Certainly in terms of caregiving, it is better for the needier member of the pair to be married, and sometimes both members benefit if the needs of one can be met by the other. However, some people are definitely better off single. Because individual differences are so important with regard to the benefits of marriage, perhaps we should not give in to our matchmaking impulses unless we are sure they are welcomed. Some of our older friends and relatives might enjoy dating the people we introduce them to, but that may not mean that they would be better off married to those people.

# 2 THE MIND

## "I'm just having a senior moment"

If asked, most people would cite forgetfulness right after wrinkled skin as
the hallmark of old age. According to the Pew Research Center (2009),
63% of respondents aged 18 to 29 believe that a person is old when he

*Great Myths of Aging*, First Edition. Joan T. Erber and Lenore T. Szuchman.
© 2015 John Wiley & Sons, Inc. Published 2015 by John Wiley & Sons, Inc.

or she frequently forgets familiar names. The percentage holding this belief does decline with age, but even among the group aged 65+, the belief is held by 47%. Why, then, are we devoting such a large section of *Great Myths of Aging* to debunking what is so obviously true? Because the devil is in the details. The fact is that forgetfulness is *not* in the category of wrinkles; some aspects of thinking remain sharp into old age and, in addition, there is great variability across individuals. Furthermore, as far as technology is concerned, we often write older adults off as being Luddites, but is that really accurate?

# Myth #9

## Brain power declines with age

The myth that brain power declines with age has been with us for decades. First, some historical perspective is in order. The story begins around the time of World War I. When war was declared, there were suddenly so many army recruits that it became necessary first to sort out the "mentally unfit" and then rank others for their ability to benefit from training for various military duties. The Army Alpha Test, usually considered the first group intelligence test, was used for this purpose. Several early research studies showed a steady age decline in scores on the Army Alpha Test from the mid-20s through the mid-60s.

By the mid-1970s, though, some researchers were questioning the assumption that age guaranteed intellectual decline. Paul Baltes and K. Warner Schaie (1974) published an article entitled "Aging and IQ: The Myth of the Twilight Years," in which they argued that it was time to put a halt to the uncritical acceptance of the idea of age decrement in intellectual abilities. In a subsequent article in the *American Psychologist*, Baltes and Schaie (1976) made a case for the *plasticity* of intelligence in the later years. (*Plasticity* refers to the malleability of intelligence – it generally implies the possibility of improvement with practice and training.) Horn and Donaldson (1976) countered this argument, insisting that age-related decline is not a myth, but rather is a reality given the evidence for the lower scores on tests that measure many important intellectual abilities.

As time went by, researchers continued to investigate the relationship between age and intellectual abilities, often measuring intelligence with the Primary Mental Abilities (PMA) test and the Wechsler Adult Intelligence Scale (WAIS). With the findings of these studies, a more complex picture began to emerge, one that would essentially lend some support to both of the above views: age maintenance as well as age decrement in intellectual abilities.

The PMA is a group test used by Schaie in his developmental studies (see e.g. Schaie, 1994). The PMA version that Schaie used included tests that measured five factors assumed to contribute to intellectual ability: V, or verbal meaning (selecting the correct synonym that defines a word); N, or number (solving arithmetic problems); W, or word fluency (active vocabulary, or retrieving words using a lexical rule); R, or inductive reasoning (inferring rules that are needed to solve problems); and S, or spatial orientation (visualizing how forms look when rotated in space). In general, there was minimal or no age-related decline on the V, N, and W factors. However, there was evidence for age-related decline on the R and S factors.

The WAIS is an individual "IQ" test with which many people are familiar – whether they know it or not. There have been several revisions over the years but, basically, the WAIS is composed of verbal subtests and performance subtests. The verbal subtests tap stored knowledge and abilities typically acquired from formal education or exposure to the culture in which a person lives. Examples of verbal subtests include vocabulary (word definitions), information (facts that adults have opportunities to pick up, like the capital of France); and comprehension (questions that require an understanding of social conventions, like what to do if you see someone fall off a bike and not get up). In contrast, the performance subtests call for the solution of new problems in new ways, with extra points often allotted for speed. Examples of performance subtests include digit symbol (the examinee sees a set of digit-symbol pairs and, as quickly as possible, must write the correct symbol under a new set of randomly arranged digits); block design (the examinee must copy a printed pattern using blocks with sides that are all white, all red, and red/white); and picture completion (the examinee must notice, for example, that a drawing of an elephant is missing a trunk).

In studies that employ the WAIS to measure intellectual abilities, the typical finding came to be known as the "classic aging pattern" (Botwinick, 1984). That is, scores on the verbal subtests generally show little or no age-related decline, so have been termed "age-insensitive." But scores on the performance subtests do show age-related decline, so have been termed "age-sensitive." Another way of phrasing this distinction is with the terms *crystallized* abilities and *fluid* abilities, respectively (Horn & Cattell, 1967). Verbal subtests measure abilities that can be considered knowledge that is hardened over time – like crystal. Performance subtests measure abilities that deal with new ways of working out problems – they call for thinking that is fluid. Baltes (1993) introduced the terms *pragmatics of intelligence* and *mechanics of intelligence*. Pragmatics of intelligence, which are based on cultural exposure to factual and procedural knowledge and are analogous to crystallized abilities, tend to be maintained with age. Mechanics of intelligence, which are assumed to be dependent on basic brain functioning and are similar to fluid abilities, tend to show age-related decline. Baltes emphasized that pragmatics of intelligence show little decline and may even increase with age. Furthermore, he argued that pragmatics of intelligence may actually compensate for any decline in mechanics of intelligence, which may decline to a lesser extent with the help of the pragmatics.

Recall that Baltes and Schaie (1976) introduced the concept of *plasticity*, which refers to the possibility that intellectual abilities can be modified with practice and training. More recently, neuropsychologists proposed the Scaffolding Theory of Aging and Cognition (STAC), a model whereby the brain adapts to any neural atrophy (wasting away of brain cells) that may occur over time by building alternative circuitry, or scaffolding. This scaffolding makes it possible for older brains to maintain a high level of functioning (Park & Reuter-Lorenz, 2009).

In addition to recognizing the importance of how intelligence is measured, investigators began to realize that the method of conducting research can be a significant factor when establishing the relationship between age and intellectual abilities. Most studies on age and intellectual abilities were (and still are) *cross-sectional*. Cross-sectional studies compare a group of younger adults with a group of older adults all at about the same point in time. *Longitudinal* studies follow the same group over time. Obviously, cross-sectional research can be completed in much less time than longitudinal research, which can stretch over decades. Despite the efficiency of cross-sectional research, Schaie (1965) pointed out (in a now classic paper on developmental research methods) that a group of people who share the same birth period (think of it in this case as a generation) make up a cohort. Depending on cohort membership, people experience specific advantages as well as specific disadvantages with regard to intellectual abilities, so there can be both positive and negative cohort effects. For example, earlier cohorts (current older adults) are probably not as well versed as are later cohorts in Internet research but their education stressed spelling and grammar much more – making them better at those than younger cohorts. Because cohort membership is associated with people's educational background, it can affect the abilities that they are likely to possess. Now think about cross-sectional research. When we compare 30-year-olds with 70-year-olds we are not only looking at age differences, we are also looking at cohort differences.

If we find evidence for decline, we don't know for sure whether it is related to age, cohort membership, or both.

But even when we can afford the time and money to do longitudinal research, we are not getting a complete picture of how age may be related to intelligence. If we test the same people repeatedly, we open the door to possible learning ("practice") effects, especially if times of testing are close together. Learning effects would minimize any age-related changes because people can improve with practice. In addition, not everyone who participates in the initial wave of a longitudinal study is willing or able to return for retesting on subsequent occasions. Some people drop out of the study, so the size of the sample diminishes over time. If the drop-out were *random and not too extreme*, this would not necessarily be a problem for interpreting the research results. Unfortunately, however, drop-out tends to be *selective*. Think about why someone might not return for a later test session (made the appointment but forgot to show up, moved out of town, got sick, maybe even died).

In an excellent demonstration of selective drop-out, Siegler and Botwinick (1979) investigated the initial test scores of participants in the Duke University Longitudinal Study. Participants who dropped out and did not complete the study were the ones who started out with lower scores, whereas those who remained in the study started out with higher scores. In light of this finding, it seems that longitudinal studies of intellectual abilities could result in an overly rosy picture – higher age-related maintenance of intellectual functioning than may have been the case if all participants in the original sample had remained in the study. Even so, decline in intellectual abilities appears to occur much later and is much less extensive when studies are longitudinal rather than cross-sectional (Schaie, 1994).

In addition to increased concern with the method used to study intellectual development, there has been growing interest in a broader view of what constitutes intellectual abilities. Until quite recently, intelligence tests had a quantitative emphasis (number of points, bonus points for speed), and test items were often academic in nature. Because younger adults are more likely than older adults to be students, such tests are more relevant to their everyday lives. As Woodruff-Pak (1989) has pointed out, there has been a gradual evolution in cognitive researchers' perspectives about intelligence. Intellectual abilities are now thought to be manifested not only in quantitative scores on tests related to academic topics, but also in qualitative measures on how people go about solving real-world dilemmas. Interest in the topic of wisdom (covered in a subsequent section) is one example of a broader perspective on intellectual abilities.

One further item that bears mentioning is that although the majority of older adults do not suffer from organic brain problems such as dementia, the incidence of such problems does increase with age (see subsequent section on this topic). Some of the older participants in the studies conducted on intellectual ability may have had mild cognitive impairment that was only diagnosed as dementia later on. Their inclusion in these studies may have inflated the extent of what was thought to be age-related decline in intellectual abilities.

Fortunately, we now have a much better understanding of the likelihood that intellectual abilities do not all follow the same age trends. The cognitive abilities that do decline do not usually do so precipitously, nor do people experience decrements in all intellectual abilities as they age. When there is decline, it tends to occur relatively late in life, and to be much smaller, when the same people are followed over time (longitudinal research) than when people differ not only in age but also in cohort membership (cross-sectional research). Decline is more likely in fluid abilities (the mechanics of intelligence) than it is in crystallized abilities (the pragmatics of intelligence). Furthermore, in studies that have reported age-related decline in intellectual abilities, there is no guarantee that every person included in the research was free of the mild cognitive impairment that can occur in the earliest stages of dementia. Finally, to the extent our definition of intellectual abilities includes real-world problem-solving (not just academic abilities), it would be inaccurate to make a blanket statement that intellectual decline occurs across the board in older adulthood.

## Myth #10 Older adults can't or won't learn new things – like technology. They would rather get a stupid phone than a smart one

Look up "You can't teach an old dog new tricks" on the Internet. Google will direct you to thefreedictionary.com, and when you get there you'll find this: "You're never going to teach your father at the age of 79 to use a computer. You can't teach an old dog new tricks, you know." Safe to say, then, that people take for granted that older people can't learn new technology.

But how accurate is the view that older adults are not receptive to innovations and that they remain attached to doing things the way they always did? Perhaps some readers of this book have never heard of passbook savings accounts and library card catalogs; they can't imagine banking without ATM cards or searching a library's holdings without using a computer. Does that mean that the old dog (your 79-year-old father or grandfather, that is) cannot or will not become well versed in the use of today's (and even tomorrow's) technology? Does he go to the bank and pass out when he can't get a passbook? Does he give up trips to the library if there is no card catalog? Of course not! Obviously, he has to get over it.

Back when few people had personal computers, Jane Ansley, a graduate student at Florida International University, was intrigued by the common notion that older adults tend to be skittish about computers and that they would be better able to succeed on a paper-and-pencil quiz than on the same quiz using a computer (Ansley & Erber, 1988). Well, they were not better off with the pencil than with the keyboard. First of all, community-living older adults ranging from 55 to 86 (mean 70) years of age were no different from undergraduates in their responses to an "attitudes toward cybernetics" self-report survey (Wagman, 1983). Second, older adults who completed a multiple-choice vocabulary quiz using (believe it or not) a now ancient Franklin Ace 1200 computer were no slower, no less accurate, and no less cautious in terms of betting "play bucks" on the correctness of their responses than were older adults who took the quiz in paper-and-pencil form. So even at the dawn of the personal computer age, there was no support for the stereotype that older adults would prefer to avoid computer technology or that they would have difficulty using it.

Older adults' technological proficiency, or lack thereof, has been a topic of particular interest with regard to employment-related issues (Czaja, 2001). Many employers expect workers to possess basic computer skills and to be willing to learn how to use new software as it is developed. Therefore, if they stereotype older people as resistant to new technology, then that is a problem – especially if the stereotype is undeserved. Czaja and Sharit (1993) compared the performance of women ranging from 25 to 70 years of age on computer-based tasks. None of the women came to the study having significant computer experience with data entry, file maintenance, or inventory management (in the 1990s this lack of experience was not as surprising as it would be today). The older women were slower than the younger ones in carrying out these tasks. However, these researchers suspected that greater experience would have helped them compensate for decline in speed. At a later date, Sharit et al. (2004) trained "younger" older adults (50–65 years) and "older" older adults (66–80) on how to use email. Over four consecutive days, both age groups improved, but the improvement was especially marked for the "older" older adults, who had started out at a lower level. This demonstrated that older adults are receptive to learning about and are capable of acquiring technological skills, although they may need more practice as they get older.

An important factor to consider is that older adults have been following certain procedures for a longer time than have young adults. Thus, the common myth that older adults are less flexible than younger adults seems a bit unfair, because they have to unlearn deeply ingrained habits in order to switch to new ways of doing things. As an example, older people almost all wear wrist watches. Young adults may wear wrist watches for decorative purposes (jewelry) but they rely much more on their handheld devices for checking the time. How long would it take you to stop checking your wrist for the time if you had recently given up wearing a watch? Would it take longer if you had been wearing a watch for 60 or 70 years? Panek (1997) contended that there is no reason to assume that older workers cannot be trained successfully, although they do benefit more when there is less pressure and more time to learn.

Technology has altered many aspects of life, and its influence extends beyond the workplace. Younger adults have been exposed to technology all through high school (laptops and tablets) and even earlier (think calculators). However, today's older adults were educated without recourse to any battery-operated learning aids, and the oldest retired before computers were used widely in the workplace. Even so, many retirees are interested in learning basic computer skills, and they are eager to take advantage of training opportunities through continuing education programs offered at community colleges, public libraries, community centers, and sometimes even on the premises of apartment buildings where they live. They know that email makes it easy to keep in touch with loved ones who live at great distances and Skype allows them to make and receive video calls. You may even know of someone's grandmother who reads stories to a little one over Skype (cybersitting as opposed to babysitting?) while mom or dad is busy doing something else. Some older people also use the Face Time app – although apps are not on their list of favorite cell phone uses. According to a Pew research survey (Duggan & Rainie, 2012), only 8% of cell phone users over 65 had downloaded an app as of 2012.

If older people were not important consumers of technology, the industry would not be marketing devices that are designed to appeal especially to them. Older adults are a fast-growing demographic for the makers of mobile phones. Check out www.snapfon.com and you'll find "the cellphone for seniors." Big buttons! Easy-to-read screen! Enhanced volume!

SOS button! High-powered LED flashlight! If you don't like that one, try the Jitterbug Plus® and get information on the same bells and whistles. Many major companies are getting on the bandwagon too. As of May 2013, 76% of adults in the U.S. aged 65 and over owned a cell phone, and 18% owned a smartphone. This compares with 91% and 56%, respectively, of all adults in the U.S. (Smith, 2013).

The Pew Research Center (2013) has compiled data on the demographics of technology use. Here are some fun facts:

- As of April, 2012, 49% of adults aged 65+ reported using the Internet, at least occasionally, compared to 79% of adults of all ages
- 47% of adults aged 65+ received email, at least occasionally, vs. 73% of all adults
- 15% of adults aged 65+ accessed the Internet on a cell phone, tablet, or other mobile handheld device, at least occasionally, vs. 53% of all adults
- 48% of adults aged 65+ owned a desktop computer vs. 58% of all adults
- 32% of adults aged 65+ owned a laptop computer vs. 61% of all adults
- Of cell phone owners
  o 32% of those aged 65+ used them to send or receive text messages vs. 79% of cell phone owners of all ages
  o 49% of those aged 65+ used them to take pictures vs. 82% of all ages

Older adults use computers to access the Internet for information about government agencies, health issues, or consumer products such as the ratings and prices of new and used cars. They use it to shop online for all manner of goods, from purchasing stocks and bonds to ordering books, clothing, and airline tickets. Online shopping is especially advantageous for older adults who no longer drive. Older adults can combat loneliness and isolation by using social networking sites. According to the Pew Research Center's survey (Hampton, Goulet, Rainie, & Purcell, 2011), in 2008, 11% of social networking site users were over 50, but by 2010 that number was 26%. Clearly, this demographic has found a place in cyberspace. Members of the over-65 age group are really active once they join Facebook: 61% of Facebook users aged 65+ have updated their status at least once; 66% of Facebook users in this age group have commented on a post at least once; 64% have "liked" something; and 40% have friended *all* of their core confidants.

In sum, there is good evidence that older adults have been participating in the technological revolution by learning at least the basics of computer use. Furthermore, according to Chen and Persson (2002), older Internet users express a higher level of psychological well-being compared with older adults who do not use the Internet.

### "Did I tell you this already?"

Almost every day there is a new headline about Alzheimer's disease. It is a worry for a lot of people who have aging parents and who are themselves aging. It is, so far, a disease for which there is no prevention and no cure. The headlines tend to be about new research and stress that this or that discovery is only the beginning of a long road toward prevention or cure. The fact is, if there is mental decline beyond that seen with normal aging, there could be a variety of causes, some of which are reversible. Thus, it is important not to harbor generalized expectations about not only the inevitability of dementia but also the root cause. That kind of thinking could keep us from seeking help for someone in the family who seems to be losing his or her edge because we just assume that it is a lost cause. Furthermore, it may prevent us from engaging older people in the use of technology or from participating in other activities that would help them keep up with cultural changes.

## Myth #11 As people grow older, they get forgetful, and this is always a sign of dementia

This belief that older adults inevitably become "senile" is so common that a reader of a *New York Times* blog does not expect anyone to take offense at the opinion expressed in the comments section: "So yeah, I hate it when people use umbrellas in the snow, except for the elderly. I put up with it from the elderly because they're probably weak and senile, and allowances must be made for them" (Hamid & Victor, 2014, February 13).

In the past, when people grew old and seemed ditsy, they were called *senile*. Senile seemed to imply a kind of inevitability, and eventually the term went out of favor – a not-nice thing to call someone. The term *senile dementia* had a more serious ring to it and had a brief run. After that, *dementia* became the common term for symptoms such as difficulties with memory, language, abstract thinking, reasoning, decision-making, and problem-solving. Now, *dementia* is increasingly referred to by professionals as *neurocognitive disorder* (American Psychiatric Association, 2013). Nevertheless, we will use the term dementia here because the majority of research to date has not yet incorporated the term neurocognitive disorder. Dementia, rather than senile dementia, makes it easier to remember that these symptoms are not confined to older adulthood – they can result from a stroke or a brain injury at any age. Similar symptoms can also occur as a result of long-term alcohol abuse, a brain tumor, Parkinson's disease (PD), HIV, or multiple sclerosis (MS). And let's not forget *dementia pugilistica* – aka boxer's dementia.

Even so, the rate of dementia does increase with age. Estimates are that dementia affects 6%, 8%, or even 10% of adults aged 65 and older, and it may affect 25%, 30%, or more of those over the age of 85 (Gatz, 2007; Karel, Gatz, & Smyer, 2012; Knight, Kaskie, Shurgot, & Dave, 2006). There is a higher incidence of dementia among older adults who live in institutional settings – approximately 58% of institutionalized older adults have some form of dementia. That's to be expected because dementia is a major factor in the decisions of family members and/or health-care workers to place older adults in institutions (Skoog, Blennow, & Marcusson, 1996).

Despite the rise in incidence with increasing age, the majority of community-living older adults do not suffer from dementia. But what about the forgetfulness we see in some of those community-living folks? Is forgetting always a sign of dementia? Not necessarily. Some types of forgetting seem to increase with "normal aging." For example, older adults with no known diagnosis of dementia complain about forgetting specific facts or forgetting names, the latter being especially bothersome. They complain of increased tip-of-tongue experiences ("I know the name of that actor – it's on the tip of my tongue"). Also, older adults report a higher incidence of absentmindedness (Kausler, Kausler, & Krupshaw, 2007), such as walking into a room for some purpose but once there, forgetting what they wanted to do or what items they had planned to retrieve. (By the way, how many times have we all opened the refrigerator only to forget what we were looking for?) In most cases, forgotten facts, names, or intentions are recalled after some delay. Even though older adults themselves may find such memory failures to be annoying, forgetting specific details about an experience and being absentminded are not necessarily ominous signs.

The website www.alz.org/co/in_my_community_alzheimers_symptoms. asp offers some guidelines to help differentiate between memory loss that may be a warning sign of Alzheimer's disease (the most common type of dementia in older adulthood, as explained in the myth that

**Table 2.1**  Examples of pathological and non-pathological cognitive problems

| Potentially pathological behaviors (warning signs) | Non-pathological slip-ups |
| --- | --- |
| Getting lost going home from work | Getting lost going to the home of a new friend |
| Forgetting having been to the doctor the previous day | Forgetting the date of one's most recent annual physical exam |
| Forgetting rules of a favorite game | Forgetting how to switch from streaming video to TV on a new remote control |
| Being confused about what the current season is | Momentarily losing track of what day of the week it is |
| Having difficulty understanding what one is reading | Momentarily losing concentration while reading |
| Calling things by the wrong name and not correcting it | Sometimes having trouble finding the right word |
| Repeating the same story over and over again | Sometimes telling the same story to the same person twice |
| Putting things away in unusual places and then not being able to find them | Misplacing things from time to time |
| Giving a significant amount of life savings to a telemarketer | Making an ill-considered purchase within one's budget |
| Neglecting to bathe | Neglecting to floss |

Source: Adapted from Alzheimer's Association, 2013.

follows) as opposed to typical memory loss that is not necessarily pathological (see Table 2.1).

Note that potentially pathological signs include forgetting skills and abilities that, presumably, were carried out with ease at a previous time (e.g., forgetting how to play a familiar game or find one's way around in a familiar neighborhood). The list also includes forgetting, or neglecting to perform, basic activities such as bathing. Most people are capable of performing these activities as part of everyday living. Another behavior considered ominous with regard to impending dementia is repetition of the same question or repeating the same story over and over again within a very short period of time. So when Aunt Sally tells you the same story that she told you last month, it doesn't qualify as "over and over again within a very short period of time." Just listen politely and don't worry about her, especially if that is the only sign of trouble.

In a recent report on data from 16,964 women (aged 70–81) who participated in the Nurses' Health Study (Amariglio, Townsend, Grodstein, Sperling, & Rentz, 2011), some older adults who had not been diagnosed with dementia expressed an awareness that their memory failures went beyond normal forgetfulness. This *subjective cognitive decline* suggests that older adults themselves may be able to detect when their forgetting is an ominous sign of a potentially pathological process.

Nevertheless, it is not always a simple matter to differentiate forgetting that occurs with the normal aging process from that which signifies the early stages of dementia. *Age-associated memory impairment* (AAMI) refers to mild forms of memory loss that occur as people get older (Butler, Lewis, & Sunderland, 1998). AAMI doesn't sound like such a terrible thing, but researchers have been trying to differentiate between AAMI and memory loss that foreshadows Alzheimer's disease (AD) or some other type of dementia. Older individuals with more than the typical level of cognitive problems are usually said to have *mild cognitive impairment* (MCI). A subcategory of MCI is *amnestic* MCI. Memory impairment is the most prominent cognitive symptom, and people with this diagnosis earn lower scores on memory tests than their age peers do. However, they do not meet the criteria for AD because they do not experience confusion or difficulty with language, and they are still able to carry on with the normal activities of daily living. As of 2013, MCI is also being referred to by professionals as *mild neurocognitive disorder* (American Psychiatric Association, 2013).

Brain-imaging studies in which older adults complete certain cognitive tasks have shown that different regions of the brain are activated in those with amnestic MCI as opposed to those without it. Are older adults with amnestic MCI at greater than average risk for eventually developing dementia? Thus far, the answer appears to be *yes*. Over a 4.5-year period, approximately 55% of those classified earlier as having amnestic MCI progress to a diagnosis of dementia, as opposed to less than 5% of those classified as having normal memory (Salthouse, 2010). For this reason, amnestic MCI is now viewed as a potential precursor to dementia. Even so, it is still not possible to predict with certainty which people targeted as having MCI will eventually be diagnosed with dementia. Nor is it possible to explain why, down the road, a small percentage of individuals without amnestic MCI may end up developing dementia.

In sum, it is not necessarily the case that getting forgetful with age means dementia is inevitable. Many types of forgetting are experienced by people of all ages. Also, some kinds of forgetting that do increase with age are not necessarily ominous early signs of oncoming dementia.

# Myth #12
## Alzheimer's disease, dementia – they're one and the same

Many people equate dementia and Alzheimer's disease, often using the terms interchangeably. Dementia affects neurons (brain cells), their connections in the brain, or both. That organic problem causes all of the symptoms that people associate with Alzheimer's disease. In actuality, AD is just one type of dementia, although based on what we know at the present time, it does seem to be the most common type to affect older adults, accounting for approximately 50% of dementia cases in that age group (Cohen & Eisdorfer, 2011).

AD usually has a gradual onset, so initially it can be difficult to detect. Over time, there is noticeable deterioration in cognitive functioning, and eventually this cognitive impairment affects not only memory, but also language and problem-solving, and indeed the very integrity of the individual's personality. Confusion and disorientation are often seen in the late stages of AD, as is the inability to perform basic tasks of everyday living such as being able to dress, feed, and toilet oneself. These problems have been traced to the death of neurons, the breakdown of connections between them, and the extensive formation of neuritic plaques and *tau* (the chief component of neurofibrillary tangles), which interfere with neuron functioning and neuron survival (National Institute on Aging, National Institutes of Health, Alzheimer's Disease Education and Referral Center, n.d.). Plaques and tangles are seen in the brains of very old individuals for whom there was no behavioral evidence of dementia prior to death (Snowdon, 1997), but generally these are much less extensive than they are in the brains of AD victims (Skoog et al., 1996).

*Vascular dementia* (VaD), the second most common form of dementia, accounts for 15% to 20% of dementia cases in older adulthood. Risk factors for VaD are advanced age; being a smoker; having diabetes, heart disease, or a history of stroke or hypertension (Skoog et al., 1996). VaD is associated with blockage of cerebral blood vessels, which usually results in *focal destruction* of brain tissue (Gatz, Kasl-Godley, & Karel, 1996). Focal destruction means that one specific part of the brain is affected, as opposed to the more generalized breakdown of brain cells that occurs with AD. *Multi-infarct dementia* (MID) is a type of VaD resulting from strokes (Cohen & Eisdorfer, 2011). In contrast to the gradual and insidious onset of AD, VaD comes on more abruptly. Also, in contrast to AD's slow but steady downhill progression, deterioration can be stepwise and fluctuating (Skoog et al., 1996), possibly due to a series of strokes, each of which may be followed by an incomplete recovery over a period weeks or months (Knight, 2004). As well, the course of VaD is not as lengthy as that of AD – approximately 50% of those diagnosed with VaD survive less than three years (Rockwood, 2006) versus at least 10 years or longer for people diagnosed with AD prior to age 80 (National Institute on Aging, National Institutes of Health, Alzheimer's Disease Education and Referral Center, n.d.). Also, personality is more preserved to the end with VaD than it is with AD. For reasons that are not completely understood, AD affects a larger number of older women than older men, even taking into account the overall greater female longevity, whereas men are more at risk for VaD.

Even so, differential diagnosis (arriving at the correct diagnosis when several conditions with similar symptoms exist) of AD and VaD is not always straightforward because at any given point in time, the symptoms overlap. Computed tomography (CT) and magnetic resonance imaging (MRI) scans are sometimes used to make a determination. CT scans can detect areas of cerebral degeneration (or atrophy) in the structure of the brain, and MRI scans use magnetic fields to detect abnormalities in soft tissue. If scanning techniques detect small focal lesions in the brain, a diagnosis of VaD or MID is suggested. Scans that detect large spaces (vacuoles) in the brain are more indicative of advanced AD. Just to confuse matters further, it is not uncommon for people aged 85 and older to have both AD and VaD (Corey-Bloom, 2000; Rockwood, 2006; Whitehouse, 2007). Furthermore, recent thinking among scientists is that vascular risk might be a common factor for both VaD and AD (Gatz, 2007).

Another form of dementia, dementia with Lewy bodies (DLB), was named after Frederick Lewy, who was the first to identify the abnormal microscopic protein deposits found in neurons, typically only with post-mortem histology. DLB has been gaining greater attention, in part because it is more common than was previously thought. In fact, it may be the second or third most common type of dementia among older adults, accounting for 10% to 15% of autopsied dementia cases (Cohen & Eisdorfer, 2011). Lewy bodies occur both in the brain stem and the cortex, which may explain why individuals with DLB have motor as well as cognitive symptoms. With DLB, movement disorders (e.g., shuffling gait, tremors, and muscle rigidity) are similar to those found with Parkinson's disease, which may explain why DLB is often misdiagnosed as PD. With PD, however, cognitive symptoms usually do not occur for a year or more after motor symptoms appear. In the case of DLB, cognitive symptoms similar to those found with AD usually occur simultaneously with motor symptoms. As with AD, the cognitive symptoms worsen gradually over time, but there is more alternation between confusion and clear thinking with DLB. Individuals with DLB have sleep disturbances and recurrent visual hallucinations, and they are especially at risk of falling. Autonomic symptoms such as difficulty with swallowing and fluctuations in blood pressure are often seen as well. Diagnostic criteria are still being developed for DLB because of its behavioral and symptomatic overlap with both PD and AD (Block, Segal, & Segal, 2013).

Yet another form of dementia is *frontotemporal dementia* (FTD), which is associated with progressive neuron deterioration in the frontal or temporal lobes of brain (Snowden, Neary, & Mann, 2002). FTD (sometimes called Pick's disease after the physician who first described it in 1892), is characterized by changes in social behavior and/or problems with language. Examples of behavior changes are lack of social tact, changes in food preferences, neglect of personal hygiene, and inability to demonstrate basic emotions. Language problems might include repeated use of a word or phrase or decline of speech output altogether. Memory problems are generally absent in this disorder. Typically, FTD is diagnosed when people are between 45 and 65 years old, whereas AD, VaD, and DLB occur more commonly in the later years. Once diagnosed, FTD progresses steadily and often rapidly.

In sum, not all dementia is Alzheimer's disease, and the recommended treatment is not identical for all types of dementia. Thus, it is important to diagnose a problem as accurately as possible. For AD, prescription medications may lessen the symptoms for some amount of time, although medications have not yet been developed that lead to a cure or a permanent cessation of the downhill course of the disease. For VaD, however, timely intervention and treatment of the underlying cause (e.g., diabetes, high blood pressure, strokes, and so on) could help prevent it from progressing. For DLB, modifying the environment to ensure it is designed to prevent falls and to accommodate other movement difficulties, and carefully monitored medications, can help to control the symptoms (Block et al., 2013). Finally, dementia-like symptoms can be reversible when they are caused by such factors as nutritional deficiencies, reactions to medications, and hypoglycemia.

## Myth #13    There's no help for Alzheimer's, so don't waste time or money on diagnosis of memory problems

At present, there does not seem to be a cure for AD, but that does not negate the importance of a differential diagnosis. First, medications may offer temporary relief of symptoms. Second, the environment can play an

important role in how well and for how long a person with AD can continue to live with some degree of independence. Third, without early
diagnosis, the success of any possible interventions is diminished. Fourth,
people who are in the early phases of AD may have a lengthy period of
time when they are capable of functioning at a sufficiently high level that
will allow them to arrange their affairs and plan for the type of care they
wish to have before they are no longer able to do so. Fifth and finally,
what initially appears to be AD could in fact be a different problem, one
for which there may be more effective treatment.

Research on the cause(s) of AD is still unfolding, and the effectiveness
of the available medications is less than we would wish. However, some
drug therapies do help many patients to a degree, and additional potentially effective medications are under development. It is certainly worthwhile to obtain a diagnosis in case one of these medications can delay any
increase in the symptoms.

How can the environment influence the length of time a person with
AD may be able to live independently? Certain environments can provide
the support needed to bridge the difficulties that a person with AD may
experience. One way to understand environmental issues is to consider
the case of President Ronald Reagan. In 1994, Reagan announced to the
world that he had AD (Ronald Reagan Presidential Library, 1994,
November 5). There is a bit of a controversy about whether he had symptoms while still in office (see e.g., Maer, 2011). If he did, however, it is
likely that the presidential environment protected him from the consequences. He didn't have to drive a car; he had a personal assistant to
make sure he didn't forget appointments; he had staff to prepare meals
and balance his checkbook (do presidents even have checkbooks?); he
did not have to risk getting lost – the Secret Service saw to that. But what
happens when an older person who lives alone starts having symptoms?
At what point does that person (and his or her relatives) need to know
what to expect down the line? People with AD need a plan. They cannot
live alone as the disease progresses, and those who live with them need to
prepare for the caregiving responsibilities.

With an early diagnosis of AD, afflicted individuals have the opportunity to make good use of the time left before the symptoms become
too severe. People can make independent decisions while that is still
possible. They may need to get current on health-care proxy paper-
work, create or update a last will and testament, make their wishes
known about who will care for them, or even take that trip to Sicily
they have been looking forward to. Financial planning is also important because of the costly care they may need. Finally, people with an

early diagnosis may be able to cope better with their symptoms if they understand what is to come.

An excellent reason to seek an accurate diagnosis when there are cognitive symptoms is that the problem may not in fact be AD. An article in *Parade Magazine* (Chen, 2012, November 11) describes the case of a 59-year-old man who had been a top-notch salesman but suddenly began to have difficulties with speech and walking, and later on with remembering familiar things such as his wife's name. Numerous consultations with doctors over the next seven years resulted in diagnoses ranging from Parkinson's disease to Alzheimer's disease. Finally, nine years after the man's symptoms first appeared, a neurologist ordered an MRI, which showed he had *normal pressure hydrocephalus* (NPH). With NPH, fluid surrounding the brain is not properly reabsorbed, and this eventually causes problems with walking and memory. To reduce pressure in the brain, a surgeon can treat NPH by drilling a hole in the skull and implanting a shunt that drains excess fluid. This surgery resulted in the man's recovery of the ability to walk and a dramatic improvement in his memory.

Not all cases are as dramatic as that of the 59-year-old salesman. However, if the root cause of a person's cognitive symptoms is poor circulation, high blood pressure, or a stroke or strokes, treatment could prevent these symptoms from progressing and, hopefully, improve a person's functioning. The cause of cognitive symptoms can be determined only with the proper screening procedures for cerebrovascular disease and risk factors such as smoking or hypertension. As mentioned earlier, there is recent speculation about whether vascular risk is a common factor not only for VaD but possibly AD as well (Gatz, 2007). If so, then treatment of circulatory issues could be helpful for VaD and, indirectly, for AD.

Recently, Matthews et al. (2013) reported evidence for a decline in the prevalence of dementia in the U.K. Study participants were 7,635 people aged 65 years and older who were assessed between 1989 and 1994, and 7,796 people aged 65 and older who were assessed between 2008 and 2011. The number of people with dementia in the latter group was 24% lower than would have been predicted just based on population aging alone. Certainly, we must be cautious in generalizing to the U.S., but there is good reason to believe that a similar phenomenon is occurring in developed countries in which there have been improvements in the prevention of vascular disease and education about this and related health issues.

Another potential culprit when people experience cognitive difficulties is medication side effects. Some medications may cause memory problems. For example, statins (e.g., Lipitor®, Zocor®, and Crestor®) are a class of drug used to control cholesterol. In February 2012, the U.S. Food and Drug Administration officially added a safety alert to the prescribing information, citing a risk (though rare) of memory loss. Sleep aids have also been implicated in cognitive impairment. For example, warnings for the popular drug Ambien® now include the fact that for elderly patients, the drug dose should be lower than it would be for younger patients because of the increased risk of impaired cognitive performance (Sanofi-Aventis, 2013).

What about using several drugs at once, or so-called *polypharmacy*? A study of adults aged 57 to 85 (Qato et al., 2008) found that 29% used at least five prescription medications concurrently – and prescription medication use was highest among those aged 75 to 85. Among those users of five prescription drugs, 46% used over-the-counter meds as well. The number of over-the-counter medications that older adults take is alarming, and when combined with prescription medications, the result could be cognitive impairment. It is worth investigating whether drug side effects, drug interactions, or both could be at the root of memory problems.

In sum, there are many reasons why early diagnosis of a memory problem is not a waste of time or money: (a) medications may be of some benefit; (b) the environment can be manipulated to buy extra time for independent living even with a progressive disease; (c) early diagnosis may reveal a condition that is amenable to intervention; (d) a patient may be able to make good use of limited time for making important decisions and fulfilling lifetime dreams or goals; and (e) the problem may not actually be AD, but could turn out to be a partially or completely reversible condition.


## Older but wiser

Here we tackle some incompatible generalizations: older people are wise except when they are acting like suckers or making overly cautious decisions. Can all of this be true? We argue that all of this is mostly untrue. First, old age does not guarantee wisdom. Second, just because they are polite does not mean that older people can be suckered out of their savings any more than people of any age. Third and finally, older people frequently make decisions more rapidly than younger people, not more slowly and cautiously.

# Myth
#14

## Wisdom comes with age, so older adults are wise

There is a common belief that wisdom increases with age and that, as a group, older adults are wise, or at least they are wiser than younger adults. This makes sense if we accept the premise that a person is not born wise; rather, wisdom must be honed with life experience. If it takes time to develop wisdom, and if time and age covary (change together), then the expectation is that wisdom will increase over the lifespan.

Before we can determine whether wisdom increases with age, it is important to address the question of what constitutes "wisdom." There is no simple answer to this question. According to one school of thought, a wise person has expert knowledge that provides him or her with insight about the practicalities and vicissitudes of life, termed *pragmatics of life* by the late Paul Baltes (who was an international leader in the scientific study of wisdom) and his colleagues (e.g., Baltes & Staudinger, 1995; Smith & Baltes, 1990; Smith, Staudinger, & Baltes, 1994). Also, a wise individual understands how the conditions of life can vary from person to person depending on an individual's culture and developmental stage. Thus, when asked for advice, a wise person takes into consideration the context of the situation. Furthermore, a wise person can offer insightful advice, but also understands that human nature is far from perfect (Taranto, 1989). Finally, a wise person behaves admirably and morally (Birren & Fisher, 1990; Birren & Schroots, 1996).

Most people assume that wisdom is associated with intelligence (Kausler et al., 2007; Sternberg & Lubart, 2001). However, Birren and Fisher (1990) contend that wisdom is not so much how much information you have; rather, it is knowing what you do *not* have and being able to make good use of what you *do* have. The wise person weighs what is known and not known and reflects on the consequences of all the alternatives before selecting one of them. A wise person remains calm and impartial while considering all aspects of a problem because he or she understands that a reflective state of mind is needed to generate alternative solutions when confronting a problem. So wisdom requires keeping one's emotions in check and not making rash decisions. In addition, wisdom requires an appreciation that truth is not absolute; rather, truth may depend upon the perspective one takes (Sternberg & Lubart, 2001). A wise person is capable of integrating opposite points of view and considering multiple aspects of complex and uncertain situations.

Jeste et al. (2010) conducted a survey to determine whether there is any consensus among wisdom theorists regarding their conceptions of wisdom. Theorists were in agreement that wisdom is a distinct entity separate from intelligence and spirituality. They concurred that wisdom is a rare personal quality that indicates advanced cognitive and emotional development. Many also thought that wisdom requires experience.

Theories about wisdom are explicit or implicit. Explicit theories are the definitions of wisdom proposed by researchers (e.g., those interviewed by Jeste et al., 2010), whereas implicit theories refer to the conceptions lay people (that is, ordinary folks who are not researchers) hold about wisdom. Lay people's implicit theories also show considerable agreement (Ardelt, 2011), namely that wisdom is a multidimensional construct that includes being knowledgeable, having the ability to think reflectively and consider various perspectives, being concerned about others, and being capable of maintaining composure under trying circumstances.

According to Ardelt (2011), Western and Eastern implicit theories about wisdom are not that different from one another. However, the cognitive aspect (having a good knowledge base and the ability to reason abstractly) is more prominent in the Western concept of wisdom, whereas the reflective-compassionate aspect (being benevolent and having concern for others) is more prominent in the Eastern concept of wisdom. Adding further to the complexity of defining wisdom, Glück and Bluck (2011) contend that even within Western culture, people's implicit conceptions about what constitutes wisdom and how wisdom develops are not unitary and could depend on age. A large sample of lay people ranging in age from 13 to 93 (average age 47) rated the importance of various items concerning what wisdom is and also how it develops. Based on these ratings, Glück and Bluck derived two conceptions of wisdom, *cognitive* and *integrative*. In the cognitive conception, the importance of knowledge is central, as is the belief that wisdom develops mainly through learning experiences and exposure to wise persons. In the integrative conception, knowledge is important, but empathy and concern for others are equally so – there is greater emphasis on how affective factors, such as emotionally challenging life experiences, influence the development of wisdom. Glück and Bluck found that as people progress through their adult years, the affective aspects take on greater importance in their conception of wisdom – as people move beyond their early 20s, they are increasingly likely to endorse an integrative conception rather than a cognitive conception of wisdom.

Despite efforts to define wisdom, being able to measure it remains challenging, but it is necessary to do so in order to determine whether wisdom increases with age. In one effort to measure wisdom, Smith and Baltes (1990) presented highly educated Berlin residents of various ages with a hypothetical family/work dilemma faced by a fictitious character ("target") and asked them what advice they would give the target on how to resolve the predicament. For example, how would they advise a young adult male target who just lost his job, but whose wife recently returned to her well-paid professional job after spending time as a home-maker? Research participants were instructed to think aloud as they formulated a plan of action that the target could use to resolve the dilemma. Later, trained raters evaluated the wisdom of the advice each participant would give to the target. There is no single "correct" solution to this sort of dilemma, but some kinds of advice were considered wiser than others. To attain a high wisdom rating, the plan of action would have to (a) define and discuss many aspects of the target's problem; (b) offer several alternatives about what the target could do, stating the positive and negative aspects of each one; (c) recognize that all strategies hold some uncertainty and evaluate the risks of each; and (d) suggest that the alternative selected be monitored and revised if necessary. Only 5% of the study participants' responses received high wisdom ratings, supporting the view that wisdom is rare. However, the responses that were rated as wise were evenly distributed over the young, middle-aged, and older groups. In short, the older participants' responses were no wiser than were those of the younger participants, but neither was there any age-related decline in wisdom. In general, participants' responses showed special insight when dilemmas were faced by a similar-aged target. So for dilemmas faced by a young target, the young and middle-aged participants' advice received higher wisdom ratings than did the older participants' advice. In contrast, for dilemmas faced by an older target, the older participants' advice was rated somewhat higher than the advice given by the young and middle-aged participants. In this way, Jeste et al.'s (2010) wisdom theorists' conception that wisdom requires experience was upheld.

Ardelt (2000) approached the measurement of wisdom by asking clinically trained interviewers to rate the wisdom of a group of healthy, educated, financially well-off European American older women, all of whom had participated in the longitudinal Berkeley Guidance Study. Even among this highly select group, there was considerable variation in wisdom ratings. Interestingly, those participants rated by the interviewers as higher on cognitive, reflective, and emotional indicators of wisdom also rated themselves higher in life satisfaction. Clearly, wisdom is desirable, but even in this select sample, age did not automatically lead to wisdom.

In sum, unlike the majority of myths about aging, this one has positive connotations, so it seems rather mean-spirited to poke holes in it. Nonetheless, the evidence we have at the present time does not support the myth that older adults are wiser than young adults. Some older adults are wise, and when they are, they often have a high sense of well-being. However, old age does not guarantee wisdom.

## Myth #15 Older adults are suckers and are easy prey for scam artists

Given the myth that wisdom necessarily increases with age, it may seem counterintuitive when we mention another myth, which is that older adults are suckers who are easily taken in by con artists. Reports abound regarding older adults' propensity to fall victim to scams. In fact, the monthly *AARP Bulletin* regularly includes a column called "Scam Alerts" that reports instances in which older consumers have been taken in by fraudulent practices. These alerts are intended to educate seniors on how to identify offers that are "too good to be true" so they can protect themselves against scam artists' aggressive and often dishonest business tactics. In one such column, Sacher (2012, October) describes a scam in which a large number of older Minnesotans were persuaded to purchase deferred annuities. Sales agents told them this would make it possible for their estates to avoid probate court legal costs upon their death. Unbeknown to these older Minnesotans, their estates most likely would not have been subject to probate court costs anyhow. But more importantly, consumers who purchased these annuities had an average age of 75, yet they were prohibited from withdrawing any of their money for up to 14 years without incurring stringent penalties. This type of financial product was hardly suitable for their age or stage of life! The good news: the firm marketing these annuities was ultimately fined more than $7 million. In most instances, however, older adults are not protected against shady sales tactics – once they purchase a product, they cannot get their money back.

In the *AARP Magazine*, Shadel (2012, October/November) interviewed a "reformed" scam artist about his strategies for convincing victims to fall for bogus deals (e.g., gold coins worth much less than victims paid for them, home equity and reverse mortgage scams, and fake business opportunities). He claimed that older adults were prime candidates for scams because they often have nest eggs of accumulated cash or paid-off homes, which this "reformed" scam artist considered equivalent to cash ready for the taking. Also, he claimed that seniors tend to share their fears and insecurities about their finances and/or health, which gave him leverage in his sales pitch. In what appeared to be a compliment, however, he did point out that the cash and assets his victims had accumulated spoke well of their intelligence – many of the older adults he "ripped off" had been doctors, lawyers, engineers, and professors.

It is possible that older people don't so much *fall* for more scams than do younger people, but rather they are *targeted* more. For example, the FBI (Federal Bureau of Investigation, n.d.) has reported a concern that older adults are targeted because they are seen as less likely than younger adults to report a fraud. Con artists may assume that older adults will not know whom to report it to, that they may be too ashamed they were victimized, or that they may be afraid that relatives may think they have lost some of their mental capacity. Furthermore, con artists expect that older adults will make poor witnesses against them, hoping that they will fail to remember important details by the time the case gets to court.

Perhaps older adults are targeted because of the fraud opportunities that are inherent, given the needs they have at their stage of life. The reality is that older adults often face a combination of health problems and income constraints, and these offer appealing opportunities for questionable entrepreneurs (e.g., long-term care insurance, medi-gap insurance policies, life insurance policies, reverse mortgages). Sometimes pitches that older adults fall victim to are not swindles, strictly speaking. But older consumers may end up wasting their money and enriching a salesperson more than need be because of unreasonable costs or hidden fees. In addition to health care, health and life insurance, and housing scams, the FBI has made a point of warning older people to be mindful of another area in which they may be especially targeted: funeral and cemetery frauds (e.g., high-priced caskets sold for cremations when no casket is required).

But just for the sake of argument, let's assume that, all other things being equal, older adults are more likely than other age groups to fall for scams. According to research conducted by the insurer MetLife Mature Market Institute (2011), American seniors lose $2.9 billion a year to fraud, and the majority of scam victims are between the ages of 80 and 89. However, although it appears that older adults may be especially likely to fall for scams, we must be wary of concluding that their vulnerability is due to age when it could simply be due to factors associated with age.

But what characteristics of the older population (other than age per se) could render them more vulnerable to scams? As is mentioned under the next myth in this section, "Older people are extra cautious when they have to make decisions," findings indicate that older adults tend to spend less time than younger adults do in considering a wide array of alternatives prior to making a decision. They tend to reach decisions more quickly than younger adults and they ask fewer questions along the way. If so, they may be more vulnerable to persuasion by scam artists who are pitching specific consumer products.

Another consideration is that cohort effects may render older adults more vulnerable to scams. One hypothesis is that older adults grew up in a time when people were more trustworthy, so that they are more likely than younger adults to assume that everyone who speaks to them is on the level. But Ponzi schemes and other fraudulent "opportunities" have been around for eons, and people of all ages, both now and in the past, have succumbed to the wiles of scam artists.

Perhaps older adults were brought up to be hospitable to strangers. Kirchheimer (2013, June) describes a retired couple in their 70s living on Social Security benefits of $2,200 a month. One day, the husband, who had early-stage dementia, answered a knock at the door and admitted two vacuum cleaner salesmen who said that they were also students at the local university. The wife did not have dementia but later claimed that she was raised to be gracious and felt she could not turn them away. The couple allowed the salesmen to wear them down until they agreed to finance a $4,400 vacuum cleaner over a six-year period to the tune of $8,000.

Factors related not just to age but also to stage of life could play a role in propensity to fall for scams. As a group, older people may be lonelier and less integrated into society compared with other age groups. Many live far from family members. Once retired, they are not plugged into a social network at work that would make it easy to check things out with colleagues. If they no longer work, older adults are at home more and thus available to take phone calls, a common way for scam artists to find victims. For these reasons, older adults may fall prey to people who are friendly to them, and they have no way, or little motivation, to check out the sincerity or validity of those people. According to research conducted by the Metlife Mature Market Institute (2011), most elderly victims live alone and require some help with either health care or home maintenance. Other signs that make their vulnerability obvious to strangers include limited mobility and confusion.

The majority of older adults are cognitively intact and do not suffer from dementia. Even so, there are age-related differences in how people process cognitive information. For example, older adults are more vulnerable to "false memories" (Jacoby & Rhodes, 2006), which means that they have greater difficulty than younger adults do with excluding misinformation from what they may actually remember. This tendency can render older adults vulnerable to scam artists who insist that the older adults had agreed earlier to listen to a sales pitch or had committed themselves to purchasing a product when this was not the case. If older adults have difficulty remembering what they did or did not agree to on a previous occasion, they may succumb to pressure from scam artists.

In research conducted by scientists at the UCLA Social Neuroscience Laboratory and the UCLA Brain Mapping Center (Castle et al., 2012), young adults (in their 20s) and older adults (aged 55 to 84) were first asked to look at facial photos selected to have either "trustworthy" cues (e.g., natural-looking smiles, straightforward gaze) or "untrustworthy" cues (e.g., fake-looking smiles, averted gaze) and rate them for both trustworthiness and approachability. The young and older adults made similar ratings, so had the same impression, when they looked at photos with trustworthy cues. However, the age groups did not agree on the photos with untrustworthy cues: the younger group rated such faces as untrustworthy and unapproachable, whereas the older group rated them as more trustworthy and approachable. In a follow-up study with a smaller sample of young and older adults, functional magnetic resonance imaging (fMRI) was used to measure the brain activity in the anterior insula (a brain region linked to feelings of disgust that may warn us when something does not seem quite right) that occurred while people were viewing photos of faces. The fMRI showed greater brain activity in the anterior insula in young adults than in older adults. However, this age discrepancy was magnified when the faces had cues associated with being untrustworthy. It is as if younger adults' brains are putting them on notice that they should be wary, but older adults' brains do not react to these cues in the same way. The UCLA scientists contend that the lesser activation in older adults' brains may indicate they are not picking up on cues that could protect them from scams.

Rather than focusing solely on brain processing as the basis for older adults' vulnerability to scams, it is important to consider that as people grow older, they have a tendency to become more positive (Isaacowitz, 2012). Carstensen (1995) contends that with increasing age, people feel they have less time to live, so they tend to look at the brighter side of things and do not allow themselves to stress out as much on small things. Actually, this type of emotional regulation characterizes not only older adults, but also younger adults who have been diagnosed with terminal illness. So the basis for the positivity effect is not necessarily age, but rather may be perceived time left to live. In any case, positivity could prevent older adults from reacting to warning signs that would otherwise sound an alarm and help them to steer clear of scams. Positivity can be beneficial for mental health; at the same time, it could render older adults more subject to scams. However, another interpretation of the positivity effect is that with increasing age, selective neural degeneration in the amygdala may dampen emotional responses to negative but not to positive information (Reed & Carstensen, 2012). The amydala is located in the anterior portion of the temporal lobe and is responsible for processing emotions.

In sum, it is impossible to make an accurate determination of the number of people who have been victims of scams because many, both old and young, are too embarrassed to report or admit it. But even if we were able to get an accurate count showing that older adults have a higher rate of victimization, we cannot conclude that age in and of itself is the basis for this statistic. Propensity to fall for scams could be related to the fact that scam artists specifically target older adults because of their expendable assets and their need for products that lend themselves to the fraudulent schemes. There may be cohort effects (e.g., older adults are more polite) that render them vulnerable. Also, there may be age-related differences in decision-making styles and in cognitive processing that could increase their vulnerability. Finally, being more positive may make older adults better victims of scams.

## Myth #16  Older people are extra cautious when they have to make decisions

It is a common myth that older adults are overly cautious, especially when they are faced with making a decision. It is certainly true that in laboratory studies on reaction time, older people can be slower than young adults. This slowness is often more pronounced when there is more than one stimulus to react to and more than one possible response. In general, age-related differences in reaction time tend to increase as the complexity of the reaction time situation increases. Clearly, laboratory-based choice and complex reaction time tests have found that older adults are considerably slower than young adults. As a real-life example of choice reaction time, think about when you are driving and you see a traffic light just ahead of you turn green, but you also see that there is a toddler playing near the curb. You have to choose between maintaining your speed and proceeding through the green light or applying the brake, so you slow down in case the toddler runs into the street – two stimuli (green light and toddler playing) and two possible responses (maintain speed or slow down).

But based on the results of laboratory-based reaction time studies, can we conclude that older adults are always slower than younger adults when it comes to making decisions? Even if older adults are slower, can this be attributed to cautiousness? Contrary to the assumption that older adults are more cautious than younger adults when decisions must be made, several recent studies using simulated real-life situations have reported that older adults tend to review less information than young adults do before settling on an alternative. Furthermore, older adults often reach decisions more quickly than do young adults. This tendency has been found in the health field when it comes to selecting a physician and a health-care plan (Löckenhoff & Carstensen, 2007). The same phenomenon has been noted when older women were asked to select from an array of breast cancer treatments (Meyer, Russo, & Talbot, 1995) and when older men were instructed to select a treatment for prostate cancer (Meyer, Talbot, & Ranalli, 2007). In these situations, the older women and men made decisions more quickly than did the young and middle-aged women and men.

Johnson (1990) asked young adult undergraduates and older retirees to make a consumer decision that many people are faced with during their lives – deciding which kind of car to purchase. Study participants could use a computer to access comparative information about the fuel economy, comfort, maintenance cost, safety record, styling, purchase price, and resale value of various automobiles. Overall, the two age groups took approximately the same amount of time to reach a final decision about which car to purchase. However, the older retirees viewed fewer pieces of information about the cars, although they spent more time on each one than the young adults did. In short, prior to making a decision, the older retirees did not consider all of the possible alternatives to the extent that the young adults did, which would indicate that they were less cautious.

In sum, it is important to distinguish between reaction time and decision-making. Rather than being overly cautious when faced with choosing between several alternatives that require thoughtful consideration, older adults sometimes review less information than younger adults do. They often make decisions, even when those decisions are far from trivial, without methodically considering all the information that is available. In some cases they seem to be in more of a hurry to make a decision – they reach a decision more quickly than do younger adults. Therefore, it is not warranted to assume that, as decision-makers, older adults are more cautious than young adults.

# 3 THE SELF

## Older people are a disagreeable bunch

A lot of the negative stereotypes about older adults are based on the idea that personality changes with age, and not for the better. Nevertheless, there is considerable evidence that the reverse is true, that personality

*Great Myths of Aging*, First Edition. Joan T. Erber and Lenore T. Szuchman.
© 2015 John Wiley & Sons, Inc. Published 2015 by John Wiley & Sons, Inc.

change is more the exception than the rule. People do not typically grow more neurotic with age and therefore do not somehow age into hypochondriasis. And the same is true for stinginess – people don't get that way with age. However, a young adult who is careful with money is often described in admirable terms, like *frugal*. When that person is older and is still careful with money, it's really not fair to change the description to *stingy*. As for grouchy, a lot of young people are grouchy, too.

## Older people are hypochondriacs

What a negative thing to say about someone! Even the American Psychiatric Association has noticed, and it has eliminated hypochondriasis as a psychiatric diagnosis. In the most recent revision of the *Diagnostic and Statistical Manual of Mental Disorders* (*DSM-5*) the American Psychiatric Association admits that the term *hypochondriasis* is "pejorative and not conducive to an effective therapeutic relationship" (American Psychiatric Association, 2013, p. 11). Most people previously diagnosed with hypochondriasis would now receive a diagnosis of "somatic symptom disorder." These folks would have physical symptoms and also abnormal thoughts, feelings, and behaviors; they may or may not have a diagnosed medical disorder. There is also "illness anxiety disorder." In *DSM-5*, this diagnosis is for people with high health anxiety but without specific physical symptoms. Nevertheless, considerable research up until now has used the terms hypochondriac and hypochondriasis. Therefore, in our discussion of the myth we too will use these terms.

Why might the myth that older adults are hypochondriacs be so pervasive? First, there is little doubt that entry into older adulthood brings an increase in chronic diseases, some of which may be accompanied by pain. An excellent example is *osteoarthritis*, a degenerative joint disease that most commonly affects weight-bearing joints (e.g., knees, hips, and spine but also fingers, wrists, elbows, and neck), which can cause pain with physical movement. Although rarely fatal in and of itself, mild cases of arthritis can cause stiffness and discomfort. Severe arthritis can have a major impact on quality of life and sometimes even leads to a loss of independence. So if an older person voices a physical complaint (or two or three), is it more likely that he or she is a hypochondriac or that he or she is really afflicted with a painful condition that has not been properly diagnosed?

Not only are older people more likely than younger people to suffer from real health problems, but also it is realistic for older adults to be more concerned about their health when something seems to be not quite right. So are some older adults misinterpreting symptoms that could just be the result of normal aging and then fearing the worst? According to Stein (2003), concern with physical symptoms can be an adaptive strategy older adults use to cope with their changing health; visits to medical providers reduce their anxiety because doing so assures them that they are being proactive in attempting to maintain their health. Many older adults have witnessed friends' illnesses. It is a matter of good judgment, then, for them to be watchful over their own symptoms and to check up on minor complaints that may develop into major illnesses. Rather than being a sign of hypochondriasis, going to the doctor with a new symptom could be a way for older adults to gain a sense of control over a troubling change from their previous physical hardiness.

As with all age groups, older adults vary in their pain thresholds, and it is usually the level of discomfort that triggers visits to health-care providers. Thus, it is important to take into account how people perceive, interpret, and report their symptoms. One person (at any age) may be the type to pass out before calling an ambulance. Another may go to the doctor with a stubbed toe. It's not fair to give the second individual a psychiatric label and assume that the toe is not broken. People vary in their sensitivity to pain, and such individual differences are likely to persist throughout life.

The view that individual differences are stable over time seems to be the hallmark of personality itself. McCrae and Costa's (1997) Five-Factor Model (FFM) is a highly influential framework within which to consider personality in general as well as a useful perspective from which to view several myths about personality in the older years. Initially, FFM, which was based on findings from the Baltimore Longitudinal Study, proposed a personality structure consisting of five dimensions, or factors: neuroticism, extraversion, openness to experience, agreeableness, and conscientiousness (NEO-AC). Individual personalities fall somewhere along each dimension, or factor. Table 3.1 shows the five personality factors as well as the traits typical of a person who scores high on each.

McCrae, Costa, and their colleagues have gathered evidence that the FFM personality model can be applied not only in the United States but in many other countries as well (McCrae, 2002). They demonstrated that the five-factor structure holds true for individuals in countries such as Germany, Italy, Portugal, Croatia, South Korea, Estonia, Russia, Japan, Spain, Britain, Turkey, and the Czech Republic. Not only do these factors describe residents of various countries, but also they seem to apply to adults of various ages and stages of life. We will revisit the FFM in several

**Table 3.1** The big five personality factors and six specific traits within each factor

| Personality factor | Traits |
|---|---|
| Neuroticism (N) | Anxiety, angry hostility, depression, self-consciousness, impulsiveness, vulnerability |
| Extraversion (E) | Warmth, gregariousness, assertiveness, activity, excitement-seeking, positive emotions |
| Openness to experience (O) | Fantasy, aesthetics, feelings, actions, ideas, values |
| Agreeableness (A) | Trust, straightforwardness, altruism, compliance, modesty, tender-mindedness |
| Conscientiousness (C) | Competence, order, dutifulness, achievement-striving, self-discipline, deliberation |

Source: Erber, 2013, adapted from McCrae and Costa, 1997.

of the myths that follow. However, the factor most relevant to hypochondriasis is neuroticism (N) – individuals high on the N factor tend to be high in traits such as anxiety, depression, hostility, self-consciousness, impulsiveness, and vulnerability. They generally show various signs of emotional distress, one of which may be manifested in somatic complaints. With regard to the myth that older people are hypochondriacs, the findings of longitudinal research indicate that where an individual stands on each FFM factor does not change significantly over the years, particularly after middle age (Roberts & DelVecchio, 2000). This means that individuals high on the neuroticism factor earlier in life tend to maintain the same relative position over their adult lifespan. If a person shows signs of hypochondriasis in older adulthood, this will most likely be so only to the extent that he or she always did – not more so with age – although the specific nature of that individual's complaints may vary over time. According to the FFM, neuroticism tends to remain stable across the adult lifespan. Thus, the idea that hypochondriasis is especially prevalent in the older adult age group is just plain inaccurate; rather, unfounded complaints, or the over-reporting of medical symptoms, are probably nothing new even for an 85-year-old person with hypochondriasis.

Research on prevalence rates of hypochondriasis bears this out. For example, in a study of general medical outpatients in a Boston hospital, 4.2% to 6.3% were estimated to warrant a diagnosis of hypochondriasis, but the rate did not differ by age (over 65 vs. under 65) or sex (Barsky, Wyshak, Klerman, & Latham, 1990). Furthermore, other studies indicate that older people are no more likely than the young to suffer from hypochondriasis (e.g., Barsky, Frank, Cleary, Wyshak, & Klerman, 1991; Boston & Merrick, 2010; McCrae, 2002).

Costa and McCrae (1985) published an important article on the subject of hypochondriasis specifically, entitled "Hypochondriasis, Neuroticism, and Aging." They discuss the "difficulties in conceptualizing and assessing both subjective perceptions of health and objective medical conditions" and also how "preconceptions and stereotypes can exert undue influence in so ambiguous an area" (p. 26). These investigators compare three models that describe the relationship between somatic complaints and medical conditions. The first and simplest model, *naïve realism*, represents the view we generally hold about ourselves, but possibly about other people as well: we take people's medical complaints at face value; that is, we believe that someone with symptoms has a physical illness – the greater the number of symptoms, the more dire the illness.

A second model, *psychiatric-categorical*, refers to a scenario in which a person lists so many symptoms that anyone would find these complaints unbelievable. Such individuals may indeed be suffering from hypochondriasis: they believe, probably incorrectly, that they are physically ill. For these individuals, symptom self-reports may not be trustworthy, but a medical professional needs to decide if there is physical and/or mental illness. After all, a hypochondriac actually can have a physical disease as well. (Obviously, this fact is inconvenient for relatives and for health-care providers.)

According to a third and more sophisticated model, *dimension of somatic concern*, there are "consistent and enduring individual differences in the perception, interpretation, and reporting of bodily symptoms" (Costa & McCrae, 1985, p. 20). Thus, each individual's self-reported symptoms must be evaluated in light of his or her characteristic style of reporting, which may be anywhere on a continuum from underreporting to overreporting.

Clearly, it is important that health-care professionals be able to tell the difference between actual illness and complaints that are unfounded. It might contribute to family harmony if relatives could do so as well. Unfortunately, it is often difficult to know for sure whether an older relative is really in pain or not. So let's say that your Aunt Tillie complains that this hurts and that hurts, or that something just doesn't feel right in her chest, or that her back aches when she sits but not when she stands. For starters, ask yourself whether she was always a little bit over the top about medical issues. If not, then do not assume late-onset hypochondriasis; instead, assume that it's time for her to see the family doctor.

Finally, let's remember that some people face new symptoms with denial rather than hypervigilance. For example, if older adults fear that their cognitive symptoms are related to dementia, they may prefer to avoid getting a diagnosis – even when a diagnosis might mean that they have a condition less dire than they feared, or an illness that would respond positively to medical and/or psychological intervention.

In sum, the preponderance of the evidence does not support the assumption that people are more likely to suffer from hypochondriasis when they are older. Of course, some older adults do complain a lot, but it is likely that that these are the very same people who complained a lot when they were younger. A blanket statement that older adults are hypochondriacs is, unambiguously, a myth. By the way, an important consideration is this: if older people actually do have more physical symptoms to complain about, yet do not complain any more than younger people do, perhaps they are behaving in a way that is actually the opposite of hypochondriasis!

Myth
#18

## Older people are stingy

"Old people are stingy!" There is little doubt that we have all heard a comment like this at some time or other. It seems that stinginess is an entrenched myth that many people attach to aging.

First, let's take a moment to consider the meaning of the word "stingy." Stingy can apply to many things, but most commonly it refers to money. On the most basic level, it suggests giving or spending money reluctantly and/or being overly careful in money matters. Synonyms for stingy include *parsimonious*, *penny-pinching*, and *frugal*. However, "stingy" has connotations beyond the idea of special care when it comes to spending money, and these are mostly negative. *Stingy* implies an absence of generosity and an inclination to be grudging, petty, and annoyingly cautious in money matters. It also suggests a tendency to be greedy and to hoard wealth for its own sake. In short, referring to someone as *stingy* is hardly complimentary.

We've probably all heard the "greedy geezer" stories that come our way every so often. Sometimes these stories are about older people who vote against the tax increases needed to fund schools or libraries or to improve roads. How could older people have so little concern for children or for the larger community? Or maybe the stories are about older adults skimping on tips in restaurants. How could older adults not care about a wonderful, deserving wait staff forced to work for the minimum wage or less if it weren't for the gratuities diners are expected, though not strictly required, to pay?

An extreme example of what might be viewed as stinginess was featured in an episode of the popular television comedy show *Seinfeld*, in which Jerry spies his old Uncle Leo shoplifting in the local bookstore. This episode has regular reruns and rarely fails to elicit a chuckle from viewers. In actuality, shoplifting is not funny, so why do we find this episode so humorous? We know from other *Seinfeld* episodes that Uncle Leo is not a wealthy man, but neither is he poverty-stricken to the extent he would be unable to pay for the books he so stealthily appropriates. So should we consider Uncle Leo to be a "greedy geezer"? In other shop-lifting scenarios, older adults steal hearing-aid batteries from pharmacies or stash raw steaks under their clothing in grocery stores. Some people make allowances for older shoplifters that stem from sympathy (see Cuddy & Fiske, 2002), whereas others believe that older adults mean to pay for items but are simply absentminded and forget to do so (see Erber, Szuchman, & Prager, 2001). Even so, many people have nothing but scorn for those who behave this way, and reports of older adults shoplifting simply fuels the negative stereotypes they already hold for this age group.

The reality is that shoplifting is not confined to older adulthood; according to the National Association for Shoplifting Prevention (n.d.), an estimated 25% of shoplifters are teenagers. Furthermore, many adult shoplifters started down this path much earlier in life. One of the longest criminal shoplifting careers ever reported was that of an 83-year-old woman who began shoplifting at the age of 6, swiping small gifts just to get her mother's attention and affection. She continued to shoplift for decades while raising a family of five and working as a nurse. She did not have a financial need to shoplift; in fact, she often felt guilty afterward and returned the items to the stores from which they had been taken. The happy ending is that, at the age of 83, she was finally able to kick the habit with the help of psychotherapy and anti-anxiety medication (Adler, 2002, February 25).

Widrick and Raskin (2010) asked people to choose between *generous* and *stingy* to describe a number of different identities (e.g., lawyer, home-less person, nurse, senior citizen, elderly person, retired person, and grandparent). Not surprisingly, more people chose *stingy* than *generous* for "senior citizen" and "elderly person." It is possible that "senior citizen" is associated with marketplace discounts ("senior discounts"), which trigger the "greedy geezer" stereotype about older adults. As for "elderly person," Widrick and Raskin contend that in general, "negative connotations are associated with the term elderly" (p. 281). However, it is interesting to note that the negative adjective, stingy, was not attributed to "retired person" or to "grandparent," both of whom were more likely to be labeled *generous*. Why the more positive label for these two? "Retired person" is associated with the workforce – even though that association has actually been terminated – which may trigger a positive stereotype. And one's own grandparent may not be perceived as a member of the stigmatized class. "Grandparent" is more personal than that. In a meta-analysis (a statistical summary of many research studies) on attitudes toward older adults, Kite, Stockdale, Whitley, and Johnson (2005) found that people are not likely to have negative perceptions about or responses to individual older adults for whom they have some prior information (e.g., health, employment and/or financial status, or personal familiarity). In contrast, negative bias is more probable when minimal information is available (Braithwaite, 1986).

If older adults are indeed more careful than are younger adults when it comes to spending money, another word that comes to mind is *frugal*, a term mentioned earlier. *Frugal* is sometimes considered a synonym for *stingy*, although usually without the added implication of greediness or lack of generosity. *Frugal* usually refers to someone who is thrifty, meaning that he or she generally avoids unnecessary expenditure of money. So you may think your grandmother and your great aunt Bessie are frugal, but at the same time you may consider older adults in general to be stingy.

It is conceivable that today's older adults are more frugal than today's young or middle-aged adults, so let's explore some possible explanations for why this could be so. A cohort is a group of individuals, or a generation, born at approximately the same time and likely to encounter similar societal influences throughout their development. The present-day cohort of older adults was raised by parents who came of age in the Great Depression, which began in 1929. Many were taught by their parents, either by word or deed, that being frugal is an important virtue. Not only were their parental role models careful about money, but credit cards were not readily available when today's older adults were in their adolescent, young adult, or even middle-aged years. These older adults were accustomed to paying in full for most purchases. There may have been payment plans for large purchases, but these were usually specific to the store the item came from. Some stores had layaway plans, but taking possession of an item from layaway was permitted only when the total payment (plus some type of fee) was paid. It is entirely possible that today's older adults have not aged into frugality; rather, they are just a frugal generation accustomed all along to paying for the majority of their purchases using cash or checks.

Hummert, Garstka, Shaner, and Strahm (1994) investigated traits that would be named most frequently by young, middle-aged, and older adults when they were asked to describe a "typical elderly adult." "Worried about finances" was among the 20 most frequently mentioned traits. It was named by 7.5% of young adults and 5% of middle-aged adults, but by 35.5% of older adults. It seems that concern with money, which Hummert at al. categorized as a trait, had especially high priority among older adults themselves.

In addition to cohort influences, a tendency toward frugality could well be strengthened by older adults' realistic fear that they might outlive their savings. There is no dearth of publicity on the baby boom generation, with the oldest members now in their mid- to late 60s but others still in their 50s. Many are caught in a "generation squeeze" because they may be working to support aged parents as well as unemployed or underemployed adult children. They are well aware that life expectancy has increased noticeably during their own lifetime, and also that there have been years of notable inflation. Added to their concern are headlines driving home the fact that medical expenses are on an upward spiral and questioning whether older adults, or anyone for that matter, will be able to afford medical care. These constant reminders, combined with an awareness of their own economic circumstances, give older adults good reason to worry that the cost of health care is rising faster than they had anticipated. As for older adults who have already retired, a large number derive the bulk of their income from Social Security. Although originally intended only as an economic safety net, Social Security in the U.S. constitutes approximately 90% of the income received by 36% of those who are presently Social Security beneficiaries. Furthermore, in 2011, almost 3.6 million older adults, or approximately 8.7% of the older population, had incomes below poverty level. However, according to a Supplemental Poverty Measure (SPM) that takes into account regional variations in living costs and items such as out-of-pocket medical expenses, this figure rises to 15.1% (U.S. Department of Health and Human Services, Administration on Aging, Administration for Community Living, 2012).

Finally, it may be the case that older adults who are not well off, and even some who are, do have the benefit of senior discounts, early-bird specials, lower property taxes, and even reduced library fines. But let's not forget that many older adults who enjoy a bit more affluence are contributing to charity, cultural organizations, and religious groups. Keep in mind that approximately 25% of Americans aged 65 and older volunteer in places such as hospitals, schools, public gardens, zoos, and museums. And it is estimated that with the baby boomers entering their older adult years in large numbers, approximately 50% will contribute to their communities through some type of voluntary work (Morrow-Howell, 2006). In short, the older age group represents a considerable source of free labor that benefits many people and institutions in our society! Furthermore, older adults who are sufficiently well off, and perhaps some who are not so well off, contribute to the financial well-being of upcoming generations by paying for grandkids' orthodontia, school tuition, college expenses, and so on.

In sum, older adults who are seen as stingy might actually just be saving for a rainy day because they do not want to become a financial burden to their children now or in the future. *Frugal* means prudent, not wasteful. Unfortunately, for a stigmatized group, *frugal* may be translated to *stingy* (ungenerous) in many people's minds, so the myth that "older people are stingy" takes on a life of its own. It may well be the case that older people are more frugal than their children and grandchildren. Perhaps because of their frugality, they will not need to call upon adult children or grandchildren for financial support. Furthermore, they may even serve as a source of financial aid to the younger generation.

## Older people are grouchy

The stereotype of the grouchy oldster is so blatant in our culture that even a movie entitled *Grumpy Old Men* doesn't sound politically incorrect. For the stereotypical grouchy old woman, one need look no further than the scores of Hallmark cards and related gift items (e.g., coffee mugs, t-shirts, and calendars) featuring Maxine. Hallmark calls her "The Queen of Crabbiness" (http://www.hallmark.com/maxine/). Even children don't escape exposure to the stereotype of grouchy older people – Robinson, Callister, Magoffin, and Moore (2007) surveyed 34 Disney animated films and found that 25% of the older characters were angry, grumpy, or stern.

By definition, a grouchy person tends to grumble and complain, and to be sulky and peevish. Remember the big five factors – NEO-AC? The "A" stands for *agreeableness*. According to McCrae (2002), agreeableness increases up to age 30 and then levels off or increases more slowly. It would seem that a person who is agreeable is not likely to be grouchy. Furthermore, older adults often focus on the sunny side of things. For example, when making decisions, they tend to pay more attention to positive information and less attention to negative information. In one study, Löckenhoff and Carstensen (2007) asked young and older adults to choose among descriptions of four different physicians and also four different health plans. Left to their own devices, older adults were more likely than younger adults to focus on the positive rather than the negative information about each physician and health plan prior to making a choice. Later on, older adults were able to recall more positive than negative information about the physician and health plan they had selected. The tendency to focus on positive information seems to be nullified only when older adults are specifically instructed to pay attention to all of the facts and details available to them.

A number of studies have investigated how young and older adults resolve dilemmas that are high in interpersonal emotional significance, such as conflicts with family members or friends. In these studies, older adults were less likely than younger adults to confront the interpersonal dilemma directly. Rather, they tended to deny a problem exists, or they either withdrew from an emotionally laden situation or passively accepted it. Birditt, Fingerman, and Almeida (2005) contend that when there is interpersonal conflict, older adults are more likely than younger adults to pick their battles and to refrain from arguing and yelling; they often prefer to wait until situations improve on their own. This same tendency seems to apply to marital relationships. Carstensen, Gottman, and Levenson (1995) videorecorded middle-aged and older married couples as they interacted during a 15-minute conversation about a problem that each couple claimed was causing continuing disagreement in their marriage. Later on, objective observers of these videorecordings rated older couples as showing less emotional affect with regard to verbal content, voice tone, facial expression, and gestures. In short, compared with middle-aged couples, older couples showed more emotional regulation, or greater control of their negative feelings (Gross et al., 1997).

Despite the losses we may incur as we grow older (e.g., deterioration in vision and hearing, and perhaps declining health), the emotional changes we experience tend to be positive. In summarizing several cross-sectional and longitudinal studies, Scheibe (2012) concludes that older adults tend to be happier, calmer, and more emotionally balanced than younger adults. Older adults achieve a higher level of affective well-being and often report feeing more positive, happy, and content, and less sad, angry, and anxious in their everyday lives.

Charles (2011) proposed the strength and vulnerability integration (SAVI) theory as a way to account for age-related gains (strengths) but also age-related losses (vulnerabilities) when it comes to dealing with stress. According to SAVI, as long as the level of stress is not too high and/or stress is not too chronic, older adults can use their lifetime of experience in dealing with difficult situations and their well-honed ability to regulate their emotional responses to overcome the negative effects of stress and thus maintain a high level of well-being. Nevertheless, SAVI concedes that experience and emotional regulation may be less effective when stress is too severe and/or too chronic. Scheibe (2012) points out that in very advanced old age, people may become less effective at emotional regulation, especially in unavoidable situations that are highly stressful.

Before we leave our discussion of the myth that older people are grouchy, let's not completely rule out the possibility that under some circumstances, they certainly can be. First, some health conditions (e.g., arthritis) that affect a greater number of older than younger people are associated with chronic pain. Also, older adults might suffer from diffuse pain that they cannot really explain. When this happens, it can seem to an observer that the person is just in a bad mood for no reason – grumpy.

Another possibility is that older adults in the early stages of dementia may still be capable of functioning with regard to many tasks of everyday life, but they may start to be forgetful. When this happens, it can be more protective of their self-esteem to blame others for missing items, forgotten mail, or for the misplaced keys or eyeglasses. If the person getting the blame does not recognize the onset of dementia, then it will likely appear that the older person is grouchy.

What if the perception of grouchiness comes from noticing that an older person doesn't laugh at your jokes? It's possible that older adults do experience some decline in the ability to appreciate jokes (Mak & Carpenter, 2007). Hearing loss could play a role. If part of the communication is missed, older adults with age-related hearing loss (termed *presbycusis*, which is characterized by missing some high-frequency speech sounds and also having difficulty in processing rapid speech) may seem grouchy when indeed they have simply missed out on the part of a "humorous" communication that makes it funny.

In sum, as a rule, older people are not grouchy unless some of the above circumstances apply, such as physical pain or cognitive or perceptual changes that may come with aging. Scheibe (2012) contends that, overall, older adults have a high level of emotional well-being, and "old age is likely to be a happy and balanced time, rather than a grouchy and distressed one" (p. 21).

### "Give me my lunch. Now go away."

Readers might be familiar with the stereotype of the older person who is needy and dependent but also somewhat withdrawn. Such a stereotypical older person might prefer to have a meal prepared by someone else rather than prepare it him- or herself. That person might also prefer to spend time at home alone rather than attend a party. Like most stereotypes, this may be true of a segment of older adults, but as we will show, it is not true for the majority. Many older people still want to have an effect on their world – to take responsibility for other people and for their environment to the extent that their health and strength permit. They would rather cook that meal for themselves if they are able to do so. And if they don't like to cook, they would probably choose to arrange for their own take-out meal. As for preferring to stay at home and enjoy the quiet life, about as many older people as younger ones have that preference. People just don't change very much in those ways.

## Myth #20 Older adults prefer to be taken care of – they don't want a lot of responsibilities

Suppose we gave you a plant and said, "Here is a nice plant. Enjoy it. We'll take care of it for you." Very pleasant, right? Or would it be better to say, "Here's a plant. You should probably water that thing if you want it to live!" Actually, in a classic real-world experiment conducted quite some time ago (Langer & Rodin, 1976), nursing home residents were given just this choice. Half of them were given the plant and instructed that they were responsible for taking care of it; the other half were given the plant without being told to care for it. After some period of time, residents who had been charged with caring for the plant and keeping it healthy were more cheerful and alert, participated more in activities, and reported a greater general sense of well-being than did those who simply sat by while the nursing home staff cared for the plant. The findings of this study certainly contradict the myth that having no responsibilities is ideal.

In yet another widely cited real-world study (Schulz, 1976), nursing home residents were visited by college students. One group of residents was allowed to control the frequency and duration of the college students' visits. A second group of residents got the same number of visits that lasted the same amount of time as the visits to the first group. However, this second group had no choice about either the frequency or the duration of the college students' visits. When Schulz controlled for the number, duration, and quality of these visits, he found that the positive impact the college students' visits had on the well-being of the residents was significantly higher when the residents were given control over their frequency and duration.

What about older adults who live in the community rather than in nursing homes or assisted living facilities? Gruenewald, Karlamangla, Greendale, Singer, and Seeman (2007) followed a sample of older adults (aged 70–79) from the MacArthur Study of Successful Aging over a seven-year period. At the outset, all participants were required to meet criteria that corresponded to the top third of their age group with regard to physical and cognitive functioning. Those who reported at the beginning of the seven-year period that they felt useful to others were, at end of the seven years, less likely to have become disabled and more likely to have survived than those who had said they did not feel useful to others.

Along the same vein, Thomas (2010) used data from a national sample of 689 older adults who participated in the Social Networks in Adult Life survey to determine whether it was better to give support or to receive support. Survey participants named people who were members of their social network; they also reported whether they had given and/or received emotional support (e.g., confiding, reassuring) and/or instrumental support (e.g., sick care) with respect to each one. Overall, older adults who gave more support than they received had a higher level of well-being than did older adults who received more support than they gave. Providing support seems to promote feelings of independence and usefulness, and being able to provide support to adult children and to friends has an especially positive effect. Interestingly, however, Thomas also found that receiving support is not necessarily negative for well-being – receiving support from a spouse or sibling was associated with positive feelings. In contrast, receiving support from adult children was not associated with positive feelings – presumably, it violates the natural order of expectations and takes away from older adults' feelings of independence. Overall, however, Thomas concluded that it is better for older adults to give than to receive.

By now you may be ready to concur that feeling useful and in control is a good thing, so let's delve into some views on how this may work. Investigators (Heckhausen & Schulz, 1995; Schulz & Heckhausen, 1996) differentiate between *primary control processes* and *secondary control processes*. Primary control processes refer to the actions and behaviors people use proactively to influence and shape a situation to fit their needs and desires. For example, if you live in a nursing home, the ability to choose the frequency and duration of college students' visits is a good example of exercising primary control. If your choices are honored, this is all to the good. Regardless of age, however, primary control processes cannot be applied in all situations. Furthermore, primary control processes are not uniformly successful when they are applied. When primary control processes are not possible, or when their success is unlikely, people often turn to secondary control processes, which depend more on internal resources. In general, secondary control processes involve accepting existing realities that cannot be changed and, in many instances, altering goals and expectations.

In the present context, the concepts of primary versus secondary control may be best illustrated using the example of the home environment. An 85-year-old woman who is determined to remain in her own home, living independently, may install a grab bar in her bathroom shower and strobe lights on her telephone in case she cannot hear it ring, both proactive efforts at primary control. She may otherwise continue living as she always has, doing her own housework and driving herself to the market to purchase groceries and other necessities. At some point, however, living with complete independence may become extremely difficult, and she may decide to redefine her conception of independence to mean just being able to continue residing in her home but perhaps not doing everything herself. Once she has revised her conception of independent living (a form of secondary control), she can hire someone to perform some of the tasks that she has always done herself but that have become too difficult, like cleaning the oven or changing the sheets. She can also engage someone to drive her to the grocery store and help her unpack the purchased items when they get home. Even though she is receiving some help, she is still able to view herself as independent.

Heckhausen (1997) proposed the *optimization of primary and secondary control* model to explain what people can do to maintain feelings of satisfaction and well-being. According to this model, age-related physical, cognitive, or social losses may reduce the likelihood that older adults will be successful in achieving all of their goals solely by exerting primary control. Therefore, older adults should be selective in their efforts at primary control. Being selective is adaptive because it allows older adults to direct their efforts at primary control in aspects of life in which the probability of success is highest. If they try to exert primary control in too many domains, some more difficult to control than others, they are likely to become frustrated and unfulfilled. Lachman (2006) concurs that older adults have the best chance of enjoying a high level of life satisfaction if they are adept at modifying what they hope to achieve in accordance with what is possible, and also if they select a small number of domains in which to exert primary control efforts.

In sum, research on control does not support the idea that older adults have a particularly strong desire or need for others to take care of them. For the frail elderly, even control over watering a plant in a nursing home promotes greater well-being than having someone else take responsibility for this task. When primary control fails or is not possible, secondary control is still a good thing. Furthermore, older people are more satisfied if they can provide support for someone else, rather than receive support and never reciprocate. It is important for younger and middle-aged adults to learn this lesson. It is natural for many people to want to take care of the older adults in every aspect of their lives and to have no expectations that they can exert control in any domain whatsoever. In the long run, however, that attitude does not do older adults any favors.

## Myth #21 Older people are introverted and prefer to spend time alone

The myth that older adults are introverted and prefer to spend time alone may have originated in the early 1960s. Around that time, investigators from the University of Chicago Committee on Human Development were conducting the Kansas City Study of Adult Life, a project involving interviews with community-living residents of this mid-western city who ranged from 40 to 70 years of age. Included in this study was the Thematic Apperception Test (TAT) – participants were shown photos of characters pictured in ambiguous social situations and were asked to tell stories about them. Individuals in their 40s tended to tell stories about characters who were energetic and eager to take risks in order to master the challenges of the outside world. In contrast, individuals in the older age groups told stories in which characters were less willing to deal with challenging situations and less eager to make emotional investments in other people. On tests like the TAT, the responses people make to ambiguous pictures may reflect something about themselves that they would not otherwise be willing or able to articulate. If so, these TAT findings suggested that as people move from their 40s to their 70s, they become more reflective and preoccupied with inner life, a tendency referred to as *increased interiority* (Neugarten, Havinghurst, & Tobin, 1968). This view complemented that of the Swiss psychiatrist Carl Jung (1875–1961), who contended that in later adulthood the demands of the external world are reduced, and there is a shift from extraversion to introversion, which allows older adults to be more reflective (Stevens, 1994).

Based in part on the Kansas City Study TAT results, Cumming and Henry (1961) introduced *disengagement theory*. The main tenet of this theory is that as people grow older, they withdraw from society. At the same time, society withdraws from older adults, expecting that they will step aside to make room for the younger generation. Thus, older adults meet with societal approval when they take a back seat, and older adults who comply with this expectation end up with a high level of life satisfaction (Passuth & Bengston, 1988). Disengagement theory created quite a stir among gerontological investigators – it triggered a controversy regarding whether older adults are happier when they remain engaged in social activity (which had been assumed previously) or whether they would prefer to disengage from social activity.

Are older people happiest when they stay active socially, or would they prefer to withdraw from social engagement and spend time alone? Further inspection of the other tests that the Kansas City Study participants completed regarding both activity level and degree of life satisfaction revealed no single pattern associated with happiness. Some individuals reported being happy as well as active and involved, whereas others – a smaller proportion – reported being happy but with only a low level of involvement. In short, what makes one older adult happy may not work for another. It most likely depends on the personality traits of the individual.

Let's revisit McCrae and Costa's (1997) Five-Factor Model, which we introduced in the discussion of Myth #17, "Older people are hypochondriacs" (see Table 3.1). Recall that the FFM categorizes personality traits along five broad dimensions, or factors: neuroticism, extraversion, openness, agreeableness, and conscientiousness. The factor directly relevant to the present myth is E (*extraversion*); typically, individuals who score high on this factor (extraverts) are outgoing, sociable, talkative, and warm. In contrast, those who score low (introverts) are reserved, inhibited, taciturn, and sober.

When investigating age and personality, we can compare people of different ages at the same point in time (cross-sectional method) or we can follow the same people over time as they grow older (longitudinal method). When researchers compare people of different ages, the same personality factors and corresponding traits seem to emerge. Also, in studies that follow the same people over a period of years, the personality traits within each of the five factors tend to remain stable over time – people high on the traits that compose the extraversion factor when they were younger tend to remain so in their later years (McCrae & Costa, 1997). Likewise, those who scored low on extraversion when they were younger are not likely to become social butterflies in old age! In terms of extraversion, there is considerable stability across adult age groups.

But how would traits and behaviors associated with extraversion manifest themselves at various stages of life? For instance, a young extraverted adult may well enjoy a large network of friends with whom he or she socializes on a daily basis. In middle age, the same individual might be involved in many hours of work as well as countless hours of child-rearing, which leaves little time for socializing outside of co-workers or immediate family members. As an older adult, this person is likely to be retired from the paid workforce and less busy with childrearing, but there may be fewer opportunities for socializing. With retirement, the work-related social network is no longer available for most people. Also, children have usually left to form their own families and may live far away and visit only on occasion. Those who were married may now be widowed. Close friends may have passed away or relocated to be closer to family members or to reside in a more protected setting where help is available on the premises. People in late old age may have given up driving, and health problems could further restrict their mobility. In short, especially in the older years, most individuals experience a narrowing of their social network. This means there will probably be a reduction in the array of social opportunities that were readily available earlier in life.

Before we accept this rather dreary scenario at face value, let's look at some findings that could modify the picture of older adults as withdrawn and preferring to spend most of the time alone. Lang and Carstensen (1994) studied individuals between the ages of 70 and 104 and found that the older the person, the smaller the social network. But even into very late adulthood, most people still maintained a network of meaningful social/emotional ties. Lang, Staudinger, and Carstensen (1998) reported that even into the ninth decade of life, older adults who score relatively high on extraversion have larger social networks than age peers who score lower on extraversion. The absolute size of a social network may decline as people grow older, but it does not disappear. Rather, there is stability into late old age: compared with those who are low on extraversion (and probably always were), those who are relatively high on this factor tend to have larger social networks even if these networks are smaller in absolute size compared with their networks earlier in life. Extraverts do not become introverts in later life, although in an absolute sense perhaps they could be considered a little less extraverted.

Now let's consider age and social activity from the vantage point of socio-emotional selectivity theory (SST). SST is a contemporary lifespan model with direct relevance both to the nature of social activity and to the size of social networks (Carstensen, 1991, 1995; Carstensen, Gross, & Fung, 1997). According to SST, two main motives determine why people engage in social interactions: information-seeking and emotion regulation. The information-seeking motive – the need and desire to be exposed to something new – dominates early in life but begins to decline in importance prior to middle age. In contrast, emotion regulation (i.e., emotional fulfillment) takes a back seat to information-seeking early in life, but by middle age it becomes increasingly important. By late life, emotion regulation becomes the stronger motive for engaging in social interactions.

How does the motive for social interaction relate to the specific people with whom you prefer to socialize? If your main motive is information-seeking, you'll probably choose to make new acquaintances and participate in novel social interactions. Novel social interactions could end up adding an interesting new dimension to your social life. However, novel social interactions carry some risk, because people who are unfamiliar may turn out to be boring, annoying, or even insulting and threatening to your self-esteem. Alternatively, if your main motive for social interaction is emotion regulation, you might prefer to interact with people who are known to you and are not only enjoyable but also bolster your self-esteem. According to SST, the reduced social activity sometimes seen in old age is actually the result of an adaptive lifelong selection process: older adults prefer to spend time socializing with those already familiar to them, presumably individuals they can count on to make them feel good about themselves. Thus, important and emotionally fulfilling social relationships are maintained in older adulthood, but superficial relationships are filtered out. Even so, older adults high in extraversion are likely to maintain a larger network of meaningful social relationships into late old age, compared with those who are low in extraversion.

It may be the case that young adults with no pressing commitments are more likely than older adults to say they would prefer spending time with a new acquaintance. But when told to imagine they will be making a cross-country move in the near future, young adults tend to select a family member or close friend over a new acquaintance to socialize with in the little time they have in their old location (Fredrickson & Carstensen, 1990). The same finding was replicated in a study conducted in Hong Kong – young Asians told to imagine they would be emigrating in the near future were just as likely as older Asians to choose a familiar friend or family member with whom to socialize in the time remaining (Fung,

Carstensen, & Lutz, 1999). In short, the social partner a person selects is influenced by perceived time left. Clearly, age and perceived time left are usually related – as we get older, we may feel that it is wiser to put our energy into social interactions that are familiar and known to give us pleasure, rather than taking a chance that socializing with a new acquaintance will be a worthwhile way of spending the time we have left.

In sum, the belief that older adults are introverted and prefer to spend time alone is clearly a myth. First, not all older adults are alike. Some are more outgoing and people-oriented than others and probably were that way even when they were younger. Even when they move into assisted living facilities, outgoing individuals will likely be the regular participants in scheduled social activities. Second, almost all older adults have a social network, albeit smaller in absolute size than it was earlier in their lives. A shrinking social network could be the result of losing relationships that older adults either cannot or do not want to replace. Nevertheless, they usually maintain close relationships with those who remain in their network.

## Why try to improve your life if the future is so brief?

Young and middle-aged adults are often afraid of becoming old, so it is not surprising that they assume people who have already reached their late years are a depressed bunch. Nevertheless, there is no truth to this assumption. Yes, older adults have most likely experienced losses: loss of loved ones, loss of some degree of independence, and loss of the ability to do some of the things they have enjoyed in the past. But as we've said before, there is no great personality change waiting for us in old age. Life circumstances may change, but we do not necessarily change appreciably. However, the fact that personality tends to be stable in important respects does not mean that older people are "set in their ways." Some people are set in their ways from a young age and stay that way. Yet, many older people think of the future as holding possibilities, just as people in other age groups do. That's why psychotherapy is a valuable option for older people, as it is for younger ones: it can make the future better than the present.

## Older adults have given up any hopes and dreams

Having no hopes and dreams for the future implies having no positive expectations and perhaps no vision for a future at all. But before we consider whether older adults have any hopes or dreams beyond the present, let's first look at what social scientists have to say about how people see themselves.

*Self-concept* is the term that social scientists use to refer to ideas that people have about themselves, or what people think they themselves are like. Although personality traits may remain relatively stable over time (McCrae & Costa, 1997), people can and do modify their self-concepts when they perceive that changes are occurring as they navigate the adult years. A self-concept is not just a general idea about what an individual thinks of himself or herself; rather, a self-concept has numerous components (*schemas*) that relate to domains as diverse as physical capability, appearance, cognitive/intellectual abilities, creative abilities, social roles, and social abilities. For example, a person can have a schema that he or she is very good at playing a musical instrument and good at making people laugh, but not very good at sports. Over the course of their adult years, individuals maintain an accurate picture of themselves by reassessing, and possibly revising, their schemas as well as reevaluating the relative importance, or priorities, of the schemas that make up their self-concept (Markus & Herzog, 1991).

It is safe to say that we have a variety of schemas when it comes to thinking about ourselves in the past (e.g., I was an excellent athlete when I was younger). We also have schemas about what we are like at the present time (e.g., I am a better athlete than most people my age). Furthermore, we have schemas about what we think we will be like in the future (e.g., I may not be as good at sports as I am now, but I will continue to be an active person as long as I can – so I'll probably be a better athlete than you). Future self-concepts have been termed *possible selves* (Cross & Markus, 1991), and they consist of schemas about what we hope we will be like (hoped-for selves) and perhaps also about what we are afraid of becoming (feared selves) in the future.

What about possible selves in late life? Do possible selves just disappear when the future seems foreshortened? Smith and Freund (2002) studied transcripts of interviews conducted over four years in which individuals aged 70 to 103 expressed their personal hopes and fears for the future. Even the oldest individuals showed evidence of dynamic possible selves, with schemas added and deleted over the four-year time period. However, in contrast to the possible selves of young adults, those of people over the age of 60 often have less to do with occupation and career and more to do with health, physical functioning, and leisure pursuits (Cross & Markus, 1991). For older adults, a hoped-for possible self might be the independent self and the healthy self; a feared possible self might be the dependent self or the unhealthy self.

Possible selves motivate individuals to do things that they think will bring them closer to their desired goal. But once again, possible selves include not only what people would like to become but also what they are afraid of becoming. For example, as a young or middle-aged adult, you might hope to be successful, rich, and loved. Therefore you will likely engage in activities and interactions that you think will improve your chances of achieving these goals. You might even have a specific hope, such as becoming a famous chef, in which case you will be motivated to work long hours perfecting your skills. Perhaps you will even be willing to spend the time and bear the expense of attending culinary school in order to realize this goal. With regard to feared possible selves, you might be afraid of becoming homeless, incompetent, or alone, in which case you are likely to engage in activities that will minimize these possibilities.

Older adults are no different from any other age group – they also envision possible selves. They too hope for success, but this hope is more likely to be associated with being healthy and maintaining independence or possibly continuing to enjoy a specific activity. Once again, hopes motivate behavior. For example, older adults who want to realize a hope of maintaining their independence by continuing to drive might take senior driving classes to maintain their driving skills (and lower insurance rates at the same time!). To realize the hope of maintaining physical mobility, they might take an exercise class. To realize the hope of maintaining cognitive skills and/or a social network, they might participate in playing bingo or chess. By working to realize these hopes, they will also be maximizing the chances that feared possible selves will be held at bay.

In sum, can we say that older people have no hopes or dreams for the future? Absolutely not! If they did not have hopes and dreams, how could they hold possible selves in their consciousness? Why would they engage in behaviors that they think will help them realize their hoped-for possible selves and minimize their feared possible selves? We cannot help but believe that older people are as conscious as anyone else that the future is coming, that they will be there to see it, and that they hope it will turn out well.

## Older people are set in their ways

We frequently read or hear that older people are set in their ways. For example, on a website meant for people about to become caregivers for older adults, we found the following bit of advice for adult children who may be planning to move back in with their parents:

Will you be happy as "second fiddle" when it comes to managing the house? This will be their home, not yours. Many seniors become more stuck in their ways with every passing year. If moving an ottoman to prevent a fall will involve major warfare, what do you predict will happen when serious decisions need to be made? Will you have an equal voice? (http://www.eldercareteam.com/public/579.cfm)

Even advice for professionals reflects the existence this myth. According to the American Psychological Association (2013), *Guidelines for Psychological Practice with Older Adults*, those who deliver psychological services are reminded to be aware of the inaccuracy of negative stereotypes such as "older adults are inflexible and stubborn." Apparently, the authors of this APA advice presume that even some professionals hold the stereotype of older people being set in their ways.

Let's begin by approaching this myth in the context of McCrae and Costa's (1987) Five-Factor Model, which was introduced in Myth #17, "Older people are hypochondriacs" (see Table 3.1). The factor directly relevant to the present myth is O, openness to experience. Being high on O would mean possessing traits such as being open to fantasy (e.g., having a vivid imagination), being open to aesthetics (e.g., appreciating art and beauty), being open to actions (i.e., willingness to try something new, being open to variety), and being open to ideas (e.g., valuing new knowledge, having curiosity, and having a broad range of interests). Recall that based on the FFM, we don't expect much change in these traits over an individual's lifespan; if so, older adults should be no less open to experience overall compared with younger adults.

Nevertheless, it is important to consider that beyond young adulthood there are probably fewer choices a person can make – there may be reduced opportunities to go down an entirely new path. Increased responsibilities, declining employment opportunities, and commitment to long-term relationships could well limit the array of options that are readily available. Thus, it follows that, as with extraversion, openness to experience may show some degree of absolute decline once individuals move beyond their younger years.

If "set in their ways" means being unwilling to try new things, there is certainly considerable evidence to the contrary for older adults. Huge numbers of older adults take advantage of extensive travel offerings, both national and international, which are sponsored by the AARP and other organizations. In addition, there is a high demand among the older population for educational programs sponsored by organizations such as Road Scholar. In 2010 alone, nearly 100,000 older adults participated in

Road Scholar programs. That organization did a survey, and 90% of participants reported that they learned something new, 85% met interesting fellow participants, 45% were revitalized by their program experience, 25% stepped outside their comfort zone, 20% had their perspective on the world changed, and 15% fulfilled a lifelong dream (Elderhostel, 2010). Osher Lifelong Learning Institutes (OLLI) sponsor courses for older adults who, after years of long hours spent in the workplace, are grateful to finally have time to satisfy their curiosity for learning about new things and meeting new people.

When people think about older adults as "set in their ways," they may have in mind a tendency for older adults to prefer to accomplish tasks using a method they are accustomed to. This could mean wanting things to be done "just so" around the house. It is possible that openness doesn't change in a basic sense, but perhaps life is a bit easier if routines are observed. After all, being open to new experience doesn't mean being open to flagrant disruption. When physical strength is waning, it might be a relief to get the house back in order after the grandchildren return home. After traveling to sightsee or visit, it might be a relief to come home and find one's favorite soap and shampoo where they belong. This is a matter of conserving one's resources, although it might look a bit like being resistant to change. Likewise, after preparing pot roast the same way for years, and noticing that everyone seems to love it, many people just might not be interested in trying a new recipe. After all, if it doesn't itch, why scratch? The same can be said for sticking with a favorite restaurant that offers good-quality food on a reliable basis. Especially if one is on a budget, the guarantee of a satisfying meal, as opposed to a disappointing one at a new eatery, could be particularly appealing. Furthermore, it is important to consider that older adults have likely been doing things a certain way for a much longer time than younger or even middle-aged adults have. Thus, switching to something new amounts to reversing a longer history of certain preferences or ways of doing things.

What about being easily persuaded? Strictly speaking, people who are set in their ways should be difficult to persuade. In contrast to what might be expected, Eaton, Visser, Krosnick, and Anand (2009) found that older adults are actually more open to persuasion than are middle-aged adults. This finding runs counter to the idea that older people are more set in their ways. Attitude strength is another aspect that could be viewed in light of being set in one's ways. Attitude strength is the extent to which an attitude is durable and impactful. Strong attitudes would seem to be a hallmark of individuals who are set in their ways. Even so, Eaton et al. found that attitudes seem to be strongest in middle age, as is resistance to attitude change. Eaton et al. suggest that social roles could be a partial explanation for this phenomenon; midlife is the time when people occupy powerful roles at work and in the community. Middle-agers make many of the decisions, and they are influential in defining social norms. As those who are in power, they are expected to be resolute, to hold firmly to their views. Eaton et al. point out that managers are more likely than subordinates to endorse having definite opinions. They would rather be stubborn than wishy-washy. As well, individuals like to see resoluteness demonstrated by individuals who are in power. People are encouraged to vote against politicians who flip-flop on issues: "He was for it until he was against it."

Before leaving our discussion of the myth that older adults are set in their ways, we are obliged to consider the following reality: events that occur with increasing frequency in older adulthood often require a change in perspective and in many cases drastic life changes. Retirement from the workforce requires a revamping of daily life and possibly developing a new identity. Widowhood necessitates radical changes, especially after decades of living as half of a couple. The loss of good friends and relatives, either through death or through their or one's own relocation to a new community or new living arrangement, can also represent a dramatic change in an older adult's social network. Finally, health issues can necessitate major revisions in lifestyle (e.g., necessary changes in diet and changes in the ease of mobility). If they were so set in their ways, how would it be possible for older adults to deal with all the changes they face? As far being able to adapt to major life events that require unfamiliar ways of thinking and living, older adults are probably at the head of the class!

# Myth #24 Growing old is depressing; no wonder older people are more depressed than younger people

*Depression* is a word that is used in more than one way. Lay people tend to use it freely to refer to everything ranging from having a mild case of the blues to harboring suicidal thoughts. In a study carried out in 26 countries (Chan et al., 2012), 3,323 participants rated old persons as being more depressed than any other age group. It seems clear that the perception people have that older adults are depressed is widespread.

When mental health professionals use the term, they distinguish between major depression and other depressive conditions. *Major depression* interferes with a person's ability to function normally. The person with this disorder can't work or study, sleep or eat as usual, or take pleasure in activities that were previously enjoyable. Most other depressive conditions are less severe, and though they can have a negative effect on quality of life, they are not disabling.

According to recent statistics from the Centers for Disease Control and Prevention (CDC, 2010), at a given moment in time, 4.1% of the U.S. population suffers from major depression and 5.1% from other depressive conditions. However, the statistics for the age 65+ group are lower than that, 2.1% and 4.8%, respectively. The group with the highest prevalence of any type of depression is aged 18 to 24, and for major depression it is those aged 45 to 64.

Mojtabai and Olfson (2004) examined the 12-month prevalence (rather than at a given moment) of major depression in nearly 1,000 community-dwelling adults who were aged 50 and over. These individuals were part of the U.S. Health and Retirement Study sponsored by the National Institute on Aging. Among these people, the rate of depression declined with age: 9.2% for ages 50 to 54, 7.7% for ages 55 to 59, 5.6% for ages 60 to 64, and 4.0% for 65+. The prevalence was somewhat higher than the CDC (2010) estimates, but that can be accounted for by the fact that over a period of one year there is more diagnosis of depression than there is at a single point during that year. Also, different diagnostic instruments can affect estimates of prevalence. Regardless, it appears that the diagnosis of major depression declines in community-living adults aged 50 and older.

We admit that it is surprising that older adults are not more depressed than they are. Their lives seem to have more depressing elements than those of younger people. Even researchers can be surprised: Mojtabai and Olfson (2004), who studied depression in that national sample we just mentioned, state that "in view of the personal losses, physical illnesses, and functional disabilities that commonly befall older age groups, it is surprising that major depression tends to decline rather than increase with advancing age" (p. 630). These authors also found that some correlates of major depression (factors that co-occur with depression but cannot be said to cause it) are similar across the age groups: depression affects predominantly women; people with less formal education; the unemployed; individuals who are separated, widowed, or divorced; and those with lower incomes.

So it seems that the myth that older people are more depressed than younger people is easily busted, at least for the community-dwelling older adults. But is this also the case for those who reside in assisted living facilities or nursing homes? Watson and colleagues (2006) studied 196 residents in 22 randomly selected large and small assisted living facilities in central Maryland. Residents' average age was 86, and most were over 80. Depression in this sample was pretty high: 24% were depressed and 8% were seriously depressed. Unfortunately, only 43% of the residents with depression were receiving treatment for it. People who were depressed were more likely to need help with activities of daily living (ADLs), such as bathing, dressing, and eating. It is not possible to say whether ADL dependency is a cause or a result of depression. These authors note that it has been argued that the two are mutually reinforcing.

What about nursing homes? Levin et al. (2007) studied documented depression in 921 nursing homes in Ohio (76,735 residents). In this group, 48% had an active diagnosis of depression. As in the assisted living sample just described, these folks were undertreated – 23% received no treatment at all. And the situation might even be worse than it sounds: disadvantaged nursing home residents, such as African Americans and those with physical and cognitive impairments, were less likely to be diagnosed, let alone treated. Thus, unless Ohio is especially depressing, nursing homes are where the depressed elderly are living.

In sum, the rate of depression in community-living older adults (who, by the way, are the majority in the older age group) is no higher and may even be lower than it is in younger adults. Thus, growing older is not, in and of itself, associated with depression. Unfortunately, however, those who reside in assisted living facilities and nursing homes are an exception. Perhaps the physical and cognitive disabilities of these older adults, which most likely lead them to reside in assisted living facilities and nursing homes in the first place, give them more reason to be depressed.

## Myth #25 Older adults do not benefit significantly from therapy

When people think about psychotherapy, why don't they immediately envision older adults as typical clients? After all, older adults do have myriad issues that would seem to be amenable to therapy – loss, grief, adjustment to new living situations, adapting to physical changes, and so on. Yet there is a myth that older adults don't benefit from therapy. A belief that lurks behind this myth is that older adults are too rigid and set in their ways to be open to change. Yet, as described under Myth #23, "Older people are set in their ways," there is little reason to assume that older adults are any less open to change than are other age groups.

Another aspect of this myth is that mental health care is a limited resource, so therapy should be aimed at younger people, who will have more time to benefit from it.

But is mental health care a limited resource? In actuality, there is no longer any dearth of clinical psychologists or other mental health professionals, so resources are considerably less limited now than they were in the past. Careers in the mental health field are very popular, and many universities have initiated graduate programs or expanded those already offered. Each year, large numbers of students graduate with master's and doctoral degrees in clinical social work, counseling, and clinical psychology. These newly minted professionals are poised to enter the field, but they are vying for fewer jobs, especially those focusing on clients in younger age groups. At the same time, there is increasing realization that the American population is aging – and that mental health practitioners will of necessity have to adjust their views about who will require their services.

Mental health professionals, such as psychologists, counselors, and psychiatrists, all have the option to specialize in working with older people. There are workshops and other training programs that enable mental health professionals with limited experience in this area to gain competence in providing effective services for older adults. Contributing to the greater acceptance of older adults' need for mental health services and the willingness of professionals to treat the problems older adults face is the fact that Medicare, the primary source of health insurance for adults aged 65 and older, now reimburses providers for mental health services more extensively than it used to.

Professionals with expertise in working with older adults have been making efforts to broadcast the mental health needs of this age group (e.g., Cohen & Eisdorfer, 2011). According to Karel, Gatz, and Smyer (2012), approximately one in five adults aged 65 and older, including those who live in the community and in institutions such as nursing homes, meet the criteria for mental disorder, assuming both emotional dysfunction and cognitive impairment are included. It may surprise some people to learn that this figure (one in five) is about the same for younger adults. Although the proportion of the population meeting the criteria for mental disorders does not vary greatly with age, different disorders predominate at different points in the lifespan, with a higher rate of cognitive disorders such as dementia (which we described in Chapter 2) in the older group. Thus, therapists are likely to need specialized training if they work with the older population.

In all fairness, older adults may have received less attention than other age groups in the area of mental health not solely because of the attitudes of the mental health establishment. Older cohorts were not socialized to accept or seek psychotherapy. Unfortunately, some older adults have memories of people they once knew being "locked up" in "loony bins," and they want no part of it. Many in the older generation assume that only people who are "crazy" need therapy, or that needing therapy is a sign of weakness or shame. For those in the very old group, it can feel unseemly to tell your problems to a stranger, and downright profligate to pay someone to listen.

Thanks to education and general exposure, individuals who are now moving into the older adult age range are more open to the benefits of therapy. In the not so distant future, the idea of "loony bins" (an image fostered so vividly by Jack Nicholson in the classic 1975 movie *One Flew Over the Cuckoo's Nest*) will no longer be the first thing people associate with mental health practitioners and therapy. Also, baby boomers will not think it is wasteful or embarrassing to tell their problems to a mental health professional rather than just confiding in friends.

A recent article published in the *New York Times* (Ellin, 2013, April 22) exemplifies the change in older adults' attitudes about therapy. The article describes an 83-year-old retired man who was not clinically depressed but felt he had "emotional issues," which he wanted to explore with a therapist. For years he had suffered with migraine headaches, and he had experienced the sudden death of his first wife and the loss of a long-term business partnership. He had never considered seeking psychological help when he was younger. But now that he was in his later years, he was finding monthly visits with a professor of clinical psychiatry to be extremely beneficial in helping him improve his relationship with his current wife and with his adult children and grandchildren. He claimed his only regret was that he did not seek counseling earlier in life. This case highlights another reason it can be short-sighted to assume therapy is wasted on older adults – older adults are usually members of a family system. They may not live under the same roof with all their family members, but the state of their health (physical, cognitive, and emotional) does affect other family members. In short, it's never too late for therapy to have beneficial effects not only for someone in advanced old age but also for the larger number of people who are in that person's social network.

What are some problems older adults experience that may warrant treatment by mental health professionals? Older adults may be dealing with unresolved issues from the past, in which case reminiscence therapy could be an effective intervention (Bohlmeijer, Westerhof, & Emmerik-de Jong, 2008; Korte, Bohlmeijer, Westerhof, & Pot, 2011). Reminiscence therapy is an approach whereby older adults are encouraged to review and both re-evaluate and integrate facets of their earlier experiences. If properly conducted by a professionally trained therapist, this process may be helpful in alleviating feelings of depression and sadness not only in community-living older adults but also for nursing home residents (Haight, Michel, & Hendrix, 1998). In addition to unresolved issues from the past, older adults may also be experiencing immediate stressors such as health problems, spousal caregiving, financial problems, loss of loved ones, and having to adjust to new living arrangements. Under such circumstances, properly designed therapy can be highly effective in helping them deal with circumstances that might otherwise seem overwhelming.

In Myth #24 we discussed "Growing old is depressing; no wonder older people are more depressed than younger people." As we explained there, although older adults do not suffer from depression at any higher rate than younger adults do, it is still the case that depression is probably the most common disorder affecting all adult age groups. Medications are available for this mood disorder, though these can have side effects, especially for older adults who suffer from other health issues and may not do well when additional items are added to an already full medicine chest. Psychotherapy, either alone or in conjunction with antidepressant medication, can be extremely beneficial (Knight, 2004). Even for severe depression, cognitive behavior therapy (CBT) can be highly effective for patients who cannot or do not want to take antidepressant medications but are dealing with stressful circumstances that could well be alleviated with therapy (see Cohen & Eisdorfer, 2011).

Cuijpers, van Straten, Smit, and Andersson (2009) investigated the effectiveness of psychotherapeutic intervention for young versus older adults who suffered from a mild to moderate level of depression. In searching the literature, they found 112 studies (20 of which focused on older adults) that compared people who received psychotherapy with people in a wait-list control group. Overall, psychotherapy was neither more nor less effective for the older adults than it was for younger adults. However, very few of the participants in any of these studies were over the age of 70, so Cuijpers et al. were unable to make a definitive statement about whether therapy would be equally effective for people in an even older age group.

We've heard a lot lately about the benefits of physical exercise for improving mood. Can't older adults just become more active instead of embarking on a costly and time-consuming course of therapy? Pinquart, Duberstein, and Lyness (2007) conducted a meta-analysis on the results of 57 studies that tested the effectiveness of therapy for older adults with depression. Overall, they found that CBT and other non-pharmacological treatments achieved better outcomes with regard to alleviating symptoms than did physical exercise alone, especially for individuals with milder forms of depression. They concluded that psychological interventions seem to be just as effective with people aged 60 to 80 as they are with younger adults.

Despite the growing evidence that psychotherapy can be helpful in treating depression, it is probably not used as often as it could be. Wei, Sambamoorthi, Olfson, Walkup, and Crystal (2005) analyzed Medicare claims from 1992 to 1999 that were filed for older adults diagnosed with depression. They found that the majority of the claims were for pharmacological antidepressants, but only 25% of the claims included psychotherapy. Also, as we noted in our discussion of Myth #24 above, people who reside in assisted living facilities and in nursing homes are vastly undertreated for depression (Levin et al., 2007; Watson et al., 2006).

Anxiety disorders and anxiety symptoms are another problem among older adults that accounts for a sizeable number of Medicare claims related to mental health. Sometimes, though not always, anxiety is comorbid with depression (that is, anxiety exists simultaneously with depression), but in some cases untreated anxiety can precede late-life depression (Ayers, Sorrell, Thorp, & Wetherell, 2007). According to Ayers et al., approximately 10% of community-living older adults suffer from diagnosable anxiety disorders, though the rate could be as high as 20% if those with anxiety symptoms but no specifically diagnosed anxiety disorder are counted. And this rate can escalate among older adults who have physical illnesses. Not only does anxiety have a negative impact on general feelings of well-being, but also it can have negative consequences for physical health (e.g., coronary heart disease) or even the ability to function in daily life. Furthermore, individuals suffering from anxiety often overuse medical services.

Unfortunately, it is not uncommon for anxiety to be treated solely with pharmacological interventions, but these can have a downside – there can be negative effects on cognitive functioning as well as physical functioning, such as causing falls. Thus, it is important to determine whether evidence-based psychological treatments could alleviate anxiety without such negative side effects and at the same time teach older adults skills they can employ on their own. There is less published research on late-life anxiety than there is on late-life depression, but Ayers et al. were able to locate 17 studies on the effectiveness of several types of psychological treatment for older adults with anxiety. The results of these studies indicated that relaxation training and CBT are especially helpful in treating anxiety.

Clearly, therapy for older adults must be tailored to their needs and capabilities. For example, for older adults still in the early stages of Alzheimer's disease, individual counseling can help with their anxiety, depression, and grief. Group therapy may also be beneficial – common problems and struggles can be shared in a discussion guided by a trained mental health professional. In the case of AD, however, older adults beyond the early stage may not be able to benefit from therapy that requires a great deal of cognitive processing (e.g., CBT). In such instances, behavioral therapy may be appropriate and also highly effective. With this type of therapy, attempts are made to manipulate environmental cues so that the individual receives positive reinforcement for engaging in desired behaviors such as feeding and toileting.

In sum, there is every reason to believe that making therapy available to the older adult population is a wise use of resources. Therapy can be effective in helping older adults to maximize their quality of life without the side effects of medications. And there are added benefits – the lives of family members and others in older adults' social network are often improved when older family members and friends are helped.

# 4 LIVING CONTEXTS

## Growing old can only mean there is more opportunity to enjoy the bliss of family relationships

Did the author Louisa May Alcott get it right when she said every house needs a grandmother in it? What about the humorist Sam Levenson, who's credited with the thought that the reason grandparents and

*Great Myths of Aging*, First Edition. Joan T. Erber and Lenore T. Szuchman.
© 2015 John Wiley & Sons, Inc. Published 2015 by John Wiley & Sons, Inc.

grandchildren get along so well is that they have a common enemy? We're not going to get into the opinions of grandchildren, but we do have some surprising revelations about the common wisdom that grandparents would love nothing better than to spend all their time with their grandchildren, whom they adore equally and blindly. We're also going to look at the clichés surrounding the togetherness of the generations when it comes to living situations. We'll also grapple with the question of whether blood really is thicker than water when it comes to late-life sibling relationships. How about this from the famous writer, Unknown: "I am smiling because you are my brother, I am laughing because there is nothing you can do about it!"

## Older adults would choose living with kids and grandkids rather than living alone

More than a few people truly believe that older adults don't want to maintain their own households – given a choice, they would move in with adult children and grandchildren at the first opportunity. The implication is that older adults are lonely and feel their lives are incomplete unless they live under the same roof with other family members. Historically, intergenerational co-residence was not unusual. In the mid-nineteenth century, 70% of older people were living with adult children (Ruggles, 2007). In many instances, extended families formed an economic unit, such as running the family farm. During the Great Depression, which began in 1929, many urban family members may have had to live under the same roof out of economic necessity.

In the U.S., there are fewer multi-generational extended families living in the same household today compared with many years ago. As of 2008, only 16.1% of Americans were living in a household with at least two adult generations (Pew Research Center, 2010). Nevertheless, the myth persists that this type of living arrangement is ideal, and that older adults who live on their own are isolated from and abandoned by their families (Bengston, Rosenthal, & Burton, 1996). This myth may be especially widely believed with regard to older women who would otherwise have to live alone (Seltzer, Lau, & Bianchi, 2012).

The eminent gerontologist Ethyl Shanas (1979) conducted a survey to determine what living arrangements older adults actually prefer. Her findings were quite clear: the majority of older adults didn't yearn to live under the same roof with adult children and grandchildren. Rather, they placed great value on maintaining separate households as long as they were physically and economically capable of doing so. Even so, they wanted to maintain their involvement with adult children and grandchildren. They didn't feel neglected by them just because they did not live under the same roof – joint living was not a requirement when it came to an emotional bond. Over half the older adults surveyed lived within 10 minutes of at least one adult child, many had visited with an adult child in the week prior to the interview, and there were frequent telephone conversations with children. These older adults expressed a desire for what Shanas termed "intimacy at a distance."

Shanas concluded that the dominant family structure in the U.S. at that time could be described as the *modified extended family*, which consists of a broad kinship network that includes grandparents, parents, grandchildren, siblings, and even nephews, nieces, and other relatives by blood or marriage. Members of the modified extended family have frequent contact and provide support for one another even though they do not live or work together. It is entirely possible that nowadays there is greater physical distance (miles, travel time) between older adults and their children, grandchildren, and other relatives. Nevertheless, the cost of long-distance phone conversations is much lower than it used to be, and technology such as Skype is readily available. This technology makes it easier for family members who don't live in the same city or even in the same state to maintain intimacy at a distance.

Even so, we are obliged to consider several factors that could temper Shanas' conclusions about "intimacy at a distance." First, certain ethnic groups in the U.S. maintain a tradition of having older adults live with adult children (see Table 4.1). Second, economics play an important role – older adults may lack sufficient monetary resources to live in a separate household or to move into costly assisted living apartments when they need help with the tasks of everyday living. Under such circumstances, older adults may have little or no choice but to move in with an adult

**Table 4.1**  Percent of multi-generational households by ethnic group

| Ethnic group | % |
|---|---|
| Hispanic | 22 |
| Black | 23 |
| Asian | 25 |
| White | 13 |

Source: Adapted from Pew Research Center, 2010.

child. Also, with the difficult job market in recent years, more adult children continue to live with their parents because of financial constraints. Some who may have established and maintained a separate household may be forced to move back in with older parents because of job loss or divorce.

In an article published in the *AARP Bulletin*, Abrahms (2013, April) describes a developing trend in the U.S.: three generations living together in what has been termed "multi-generational housing" or "multigen housing." Abrahms refers to statistics collected by the Pew Research Center (2011), which are based on U.S. Census Bureau data: 51 million Americans (16.7% of the population) presently live in a house with at least two adult generations, and multi-generational households increased by 10.5% from 2007 to 2009. Abrahms also notes that 61% of Americans aged 25 to 34 have friends or family members who have had to move back in with parents or other relatives because they have no job, no money, and no other place to live. Some of the nation's biggest homebuilders, aware of this growing trend, have responded by introducing housing with floor plans with more than one master suite and/or flexible space such as a family room that can be converted into a bedroom and bathroom. In some instances, adult children and their elderly parents have combined resources to purchase a "Nex Gen" concept home, which is actually two homes in one – a main home as well as a smaller attached unit with its own entrance, kitchen, bedroom, living space, and garage. These arrangements can be helpful if several generations plan to live together. However, Abrahms does acknowledge that multigen living is not always ideal – it is not without family friction, and it can put a strain on marriages.

In general, older adults want to remain in contact with adult children and grandchildren, but they also enjoy spending time with friends (Connidis, 1989). Friendship is voluntary and there are no formal rules, so older adults can select friends with whom they have common interests without being bound to them by duty. As long as relationships with friends are reciprocal, older adults can enjoy both giving and receiving various types of support, and having a friendship network helps them maintain a sense of independence (Rook, 1987). Friends may do favors and offer to help one another on a short-term basis (Connidis, 1989). But when older adults begin to need a great deal of help, especially when it is not likely that they will ever be able to reciprocate, they usually turn to family members. This often happens when an older adult has been living independently but then develops a serious illness or begins to need considerable assistance with instrumental activities of daily living such as shopping, cooking, and paying bills. If the need for assistance is expected to continue for a long period of time, there is little chance the older adult will ever be able to reciprocate when the friends who are helping start to need help themselves. At this point, adult children or other family members are usually called in, and some arrangement is made to care for the older family member.

One of your authors knows an affluent older woman who lives independently and whose adult son lives at a considerable distance. When neighbors noticed that she was experiencing cognitive problems that interfered with her daily living, her son was alerted. When he visited, he hired a "companion" to look in on her and accompany her to appointments and leisure activities, such as meals in restaurants. Not all older adults have the financial resources for such an arrangement; some may have to move in with adult children or other relatives if they cannot continue to live on their own. This is especially likely to happen when financial resources are not sufficient for the older adult to pay for an assisted living arrangement.

In sum, with the exception of certain cultural groups that have a tradition of multi-generational households, many older adults want to maintain their own living space as long as they are able to do so. But this certainly does not mean that they don't want to have contact with family members.

## Myth #27 Older adults want to spend all their time with grandkids and they never have favorites

Let's start by acknowledging that most people are thrilled when the first grandchild arrives. In fact, they're usually thrilled with the birth of the second, third, and even the tenth grandchild as well. They fall in love with those new babies just as they did with their own babies. But something different happens with grandchildren: the birth of a grandchild heralds a new generation, which reinforces family solidarity and a sense of family lineage that will go on and on. Nevertheless, even if the emotions are the same each time a new grandchild is born, the grandparent role can vary considerably, and the relationship is not necessarily identical with every grandchild.

A number of factors can influence grandparent/grandchild roles and relationships. In general, the grandparents' age and stage of life can make a difference. In some cases, grandparents still work full-time and don't have much time to spend with grandchildren compared with grandparents who are retired and have more leisure time. Among grandparents who are retired, those in good health are likely to spend more time with grandchildren compared with those in poor health. Grandparents who live in the same locale are likely to see grandchildren more compared with those who live afar. But we know a set of grandparents who board an airplane every month so they can spend up to two weeks with grandchildren. Perhaps our readers know of similarly devoted grandparents. Also, though this is not the norm, some young grandparents have babies or young children of their own and therefore have less time to devote to their grandchildren.

The marital status of grandparents can play a part in their relationships with grandchildren. For example, a grandparent who remarries after becoming widowed or divorced may spend less time with and be less close to grandchildren. Also, grandparents whose adult children have blended families are likely to be in a more complex situation and may have to allocate their time and attention to step-grandchildren as well as grandchildren. In addition, age of grandchildren is a factor; grandparents usually have a closer relationship when grandchildren are young than when they grow older (Fingerman, 2004).

Kivnick and Sinclair (1996) identified three grandparenting styles: remote, companionate, and involved. *Remote grandparents* are emotionally distant and formal. Many live far from grandchildren or are busy with work or other interests. *Companionate grandparents*, probably the most common style in contemporary American society, engage in entertaining and pleasurable leisure activities with grandchildren. In general, however, they avoid interfering in the discipline of grandchildren, leaving it to the parents. Perhaps this is a wise strategy, given the negative attitudes, particularly among middle-class European American mothers, toward grandparents who give unsolicited advice about child-rearing (Norris & Tindale, 1994; Thomas, 1990). In the article on multi-generational housing, Abrahms (2013, April) points out that a potential downside is that grandparents may be viewed as interfering in the rearing of grandchildren when they all live in the same home. On the contrary, advice from grandparents may be more acceptable in African American and Asian American families, especially when the grandparents live in the same household (Norris & Tindale, 1994). *Involved grandparents* spend a great deal of time with grandchildren, in some instances caring for them full-time while their parents work outside the home.

With the high divorce rate as well as the difficult economy, parents of young children must often work, and sometimes they turn to grandparents to assist with childcare. In urban African American families, grandmothers are often responsible for rearing grandchildren, especially if the grandchildren's mother is a single parent. Across all ethnic and economic groups, however, custodial grandparents who care for grandchildren on a full-time basis are becoming more prevalent. Sadly, grandparents may function as surrogate parents when adult children are deceased or otherwise unable to fulfill the parental role because of substance abuse or problems with mental or physical health. According to the American Community Survey (Murphey, Cooper, & Moore, 2012), the number of children living in a home headed by a grandparent rose from 4.6 million in 2005–2007 to 5.2 million in 2008–2010. That's about 7% of all children in the U.S. Furthermore, the age distribution of these children was slightly younger in 2008–2010 than previously.

This trend is so important that innovative housing for grandparents who are raising grandchildren is being developed all over the country. For example, a Chicago-based non-profit organization set up a senior campus with three types of buildings: affordable apartments, assisted living facilities, and apartments for grandfamilies. There are on-site social workers, a nearby after-school program, and even a foster parent arrangement whereby grandparents who need to move into assisted living can do so but grandchildren can remain in place (Adler, 2007, June 3).

Grandparents do not necessarily have the same relationship with all of their grandchildren, and they tend to be less invested in any given grandchild when there are large numbers of grandchildren. Overall, compared with grandfathers, grandmothers tend to be more invested in and to enjoy time spent with grandchildren (Fingerman, 1998, 2004). Even so, the strength of ties to grandchildren is dependent to some extent on the relationship of the older generation with the middle generation, or the grandchildren's parents (Fingerman, 2004; Giarrusso & Silverstein, 1995). The quality of the grandparents' relationships with in-laws (especially daughters-in-law) seems to play an especially important role in their ties to and enjoyment of the grandchildren.

It is often assumed that grandparents have similar feelings toward all of their grandchildren. Certainly, expressing an outright preference for one grandchild over another is not something about which grandparents speak freely. But there may be some preference depending on a grandchild's age, gender, or birth order. Also, grandparents may feel closer to a grandchild who shares the same religion than to one who does not, or to a grandchild who has personal attributes of which they approve (e.g., a high level of achievement). Grandparents may consider a particular grandchild to be special in a positive way. In contrast, however, they may find the behavior of another grandchild to be irritating. They may feel frustrated and helpless if they think a grandchild has problems or difficulties, and they may worry about how that grandchild will turn out down the road.

In sum, being a grandparent is not a unitary role. The relationship between grandparents and grandchildren is influenced by a variety of factors and can take many forms. Many factors come into play when delineating the type of relationship grandparents have with individual grandchildren and also how they feel about each grandchild.

## Sibling relationships are stable throughout life

It is often taken for granted that sibling relationships remain pretty much the same over the lifespan, but in reality this is not the case. What is the nature of sibling relationships, and how do they actually evolve over time?

There are no firm societal rules or formal guidelines about sibling relationships, probably because families come in many different forms and family dynamics can vary along so many dimensions. How many siblings did you have as you were growing up? Did you have sisters and/ or brothers? What about birth order – were you the oldest, the youngest, or something in between? What is the age difference between you and your siblings? Were parental expectations the same for all siblings, or were some given more responsibility and others granted greater privileges?

Despite the diversity among families, researchers (e.g., Norris & Tindale, 1994) have suggested that, over time, there is an *hourglass effect* in sibling relationships. Sibling relationships are closest in the younger growing-up years; they become constricted in early and middle adulthood, but then they move toward greater closeness in late middle age and older adulthood.

In their early years, siblings typically live with the family they were born into (family of origin), which serves to foster closeness. That is not to say siblings never argue or fight physically; such behavior could actually signify a form of closeness fostered by a set of common circumstances. As siblings grow older, their lives begin to diverge. Upon high school graduation, some continue on to a college or university, whereas others enter the workforce. Of those who pursue higher education, some attend schools in their hometown and continue to live in the family home. Others physically leave their family of origin to attend institutions in new cities or states. When they graduate, they may remain in the same locale where they attended school, or perhaps they relocate to a city or area of the country that offers employment opportunities. Marriage is another factor that can determine where people live; some individuals migrate to a new geographical area because of a spouse or significant other. Perhaps because of the differing paths siblings' lives can take, sibling relationships that were once close may not remain so.

As time goes by, young and middle-aged adults typically pursue careers that require long hours of work, sometimes at a considerable distance from siblings. Many marry and form their own families. At this stage of life, the time and money needed for sibling get-togethers can be prohibitive. Also, with marriage there is not only a spouse but also a second set of extended family members, leaving less time for siblings. It should not be surprising, then, that siblings tend to drift apart in the middle years. Nevertheless, siblings often grow closer later in life for several reasons. First, their children are likely to be grown and to have flown the nest, leaving more time for the parents to get together with siblings. Once children are launched, siblings may have more financial resources for visits to brothers and sisters who live at a distance. Careers may have peaked, with plans for retirement in the works.

Another factor that can bring siblings closer is widowhood or even divorce. For siblings in long-term marriages, the spousal relationship usually predominates, leaving less time for sibling relationships, especially if siblings live at a distance. Also, if a brother or sister marries someone who is not pleasant, friendly, or accepting of other family members, there could well be obstacles to siblings' remaining close. But if, down the road, that sibling becomes divorced or widowed, sibling closeness may resume.

One further factor that can lead to increased sibling closeness is that as individuals move into the later years, their common background becomes more meaningful. Also, as members of the oldest generation (i.e., parents but possibly other relatives such as aunts and uncles) begin to need help in some form, siblings must often get together to plan the best strategy for providing the necessary aid. Siblings may find it necessary to interact frequently over concern for elderly parents. For many siblings, getting together in late middle age or early older adulthood over shared concerns for aging parents strengthens their feelings of closeness. However, if siblings harbor resentment over earlier family dynamics or conflicts that were never resolved, negative feelings could flare up when they're forced to reunite over caregiving for aging parents (Bengston et al., 1996; Connidis, 1994). Also, it often happens that the sibling who lives closest shoulders the responsibility for the aging parent. This sibling may resent brothers and sisters who live far away but make no apparent effort to help out with regular visits or financial contributions when these are needed. The resentment felt by the sibling with the caregiving responsibility can be especially intense if he or she feels that a brother or sister was always favored by the parent.

The hourglass effect describes the trajectory of many sibling relationships, but it is important to recognize that not all sibling relationships fit the identical pattern. Gold (1989, 1990) studied samples of both European American and African American late-life sibling dyads and identified five categories of late-life sibling relationships. These categories fall on a continuum from a greater to a lesser degree of emotional closeness, respectively, as follows: intimate, congenial, loyal, apathetic, and hostile. In general, sibling relationships were closer among African Americans than they were among European Americans. Also, sibling dyads that included a sister (either two sisters or a brother and a sister) clustered in the more positive categories, whereas dyads composed of two brothers tended to have less involvement.

An important aspect of late-life sibling relationships is the extent to which siblings say they would provide support for one another in times of crisis or stress. Relationships with siblings are less defined than those with spouses and children, so such behavior is generally considered to be more voluntary (Bengston et al., 1996). According to the *hierarchical-compensatory model* (Cantor, 1979), individuals have a hierarchy of relationships that determines whom they call upon for support in a time of need. When a spouse or adult children are not available because of death, divorce, or geographical distance, older adults may turn to siblings, who are lower down in the hierarchy. This hierarchical-compensatory model could explain why sibling support is stronger among older adults who are single or widowed, and childless, than it is among older adults who are married and have adult children.

Connidis (1994) conducted a survey of Canadians over the age of 55 and found marital status was an important determinant when it comes to sibling support. Compared with individuals who were married, those who were widowed were more likely to receive sibling support during an illness and on a long-term basis if needed. Those who were widowed or divorced were more likely than those who were married to say that they would provide shelter for a sibling if necessary. Nevertheless, unless siblings already have a reciprocal relationship whereby they help one another on a regular basis, support from a sibling is usually temporary (Cicirelli, 1995).

What other factors determine whether siblings step up to the plate when a brother or sister needs help in a time of need? Number of siblings seems to make a difference: support is more likely when an individual has two or more siblings rather than only one (Connidis, 1994). It's not clear why having only one sibling is a disadvantage, even when the actual support is often supplied by only one sibling. It's possible that one sibling's efforts result from active negotiation among all of the siblings, who reach an agreement over who will be responsible for helping a brother or sister in need. In addition to having two or more siblings, having a sister is a definite advantage – those with sisters were more likely to think they would receive support during a crisis than those with only brothers. It may well be that women tend to maintain stronger ties than men do to their family of origin. Men may have a closer attachment to their wife's family of origin, including her siblings, than to their own family of origin (Bengston et al., 1996).

In sum, sibling relationships do not remain frozen over time. Relationships that were close early in life often drift apart. But in late middle age or early older adulthood, sibling relationships may once again flourish. Ideally, siblings become closer when faced with making decisions about care of the older generation. Late-life sibling relationships will probably take on greater significance in the not too distant future because the rate of divorce is higher today than in decades past. Also, married couples are having fewer children, so siblings could well become a more important source of closeness and support for older adults than they are now.

## Retirement is for sissies

Do older workers count the days till they can retire, or do they want to keep working until they drop? Once they do retire, are they eager to get to where they can play golf year round? Or is it more accurate to assume that they resist retirement and refuse to make space for younger workers? One view has it that older people lose their edge and should retire, but they hesitate to do so because they're afraid that it will be depressing, or perhaps they are just plain greedy. Also, many people think that older adults can always get work if they want to, so in a difficult economy they always seem to crowd out the young workers. By contrast, some people believe that retirement seems like easy street: lots of financial benefits and warm weather are waiting. Here we will discuss what research has to say about the effectiveness of older workers and the status of the laws relating to workplace discrimination against them. Then we'll delve into the myths about retirement – who enjoys it, who can afford it, and who is moving to the Sunbelt.

# Older workers are inferior to younger workers

A common myth is that older employees are much less desirable than younger ones. Even the American Psychological Association advises psychologists to beware of the stereotype that older adults are inefficient in the workplace (American Psychological Association, 2013). There are several aspects to this myth. First, there is the assumption that older employees are less competent than younger ones (e.g., they're slow, unable to learn or use new technology). Second, there is a belief that older workers are unreliable and bound to take more days off from work than younger workers. Finally, it is often taken for granted that, due to their age, older workers will not last long with the organization. But what do we actually know about older employees?

With regard to competency, jobs vary in their requirements. Some jobs require extensive knowledge about technology. It's generally the case that the present-day older cohort is not well versed in the use of technology compared with younger cohorts, who probably started using it in their school years or even earlier. Nevertheless, in an early study conducted long before "Google" became a household word, Ansley and Erber (1988) demonstrated that older adults had a positive attitude toward computers and were fully capable of using them. It may take more time to train older adults because they are not as accustomed to using technology as younger adults are. For the most part, however, older adults are willing and able to learn (Sharit et al., 2004). In the coming years, cohorts moving into their mature years will have more extensive technological background and experience – this is already occurring – so it will not take much effort for them to adapt to nuances that are constantly changing.

Important as it is for some jobs, technology is not the prime consideration for all types of employment. Older adults are generally just as capable as younger adults, perhaps even more so, when jobs call for social skills and a store of wisdom and relevant experience (crystallized abilities), which are discussed in more detail under Myth #9, "Brain power declines with age" (Bowen, Noack, & Staudinger, 2011). Also, older adults are just as vigilant as younger adults, that is, capable of the monitoring that is necessary in order to detect errors (Kausler, Kausler, & Krupshaw, 2007). Nevertheless, in highly complex situations that call for keeping track of a large number of tasks at the same time, older adults may be moderately less accurate than younger adults (Kausler et al., 2007; Rogers & Fisk, 2001). Although speed of processing may decline with age, it can often be remedied with practice and training. And for many jobs, accumulated knowledge and experience can compensate for any decline in speed (Cleveland & Shore, 2007; Salthouse & Maurer, 1996). In jobs that allow employees to process tasks sequentially (as opposed to multitasking), especially when accuracy is valued more than speed, older workers can certainly compete with younger ones.

As to the assumption that older employees are unreliable, the reality is that they have a lower rate of absenteeism than younger employees do (Panek, 1997). Older workers tend to be highly committed to their jobs. They have a great deal of investment in the work role and express greater job satisfaction than younger workers do (Ekerdt & DeViney, 1993). Their satisfaction seems to be especially high in human service jobs (Cleveland & Shore, 2007). It's also important to consider what the Towers Watson Global Workforce Study (2012) calls *presenteeism* – lost productivity at work. This refers to a situation we are all familiar with: one can be present at work but not be working very hard. Perhaps more gets done than when we don't go to work at all, but this sort of lost work time can add up. We can infer that older adults, by being highly committed to their jobs and by having a big investment in their role as workers, would also be more engaged in their work, and thus have lower presenteeism than many younger workers. According to this study, highly engaged employees have lower presenteeism as well as less absenteeism than disengaged employees.

Now let's turn to the belief many people have that, once hired, older employees will not last as long with the organization as younger employees will. Indeed, younger adults probably have more years of full-time employment ahead of them than older adults do. But the years younger adults spend toiling in the workplace will not necessarily all be with the same employer. Younger employees are *more* likely than older ones to move on to other jobs, partly because they are at the stage in their career trajectory where they are searching for the "ideal" job. Given the culture of the contemporary American workplace, changing employers is often the route to salary increases and promotions, which are especially attractive to younger employees, many of whom are starting families and in need of a higher income. In addition, many younger adults enter the workplace with student loan debt, so their financial needs motivate them to search for jobs that offer higher salaries. In contrast, older employees' positive attitudes and job satisfaction mean they are likely to stick with an employer longer than younger employees will.

In sum, there's abundant evidence to bust the myth that as workers, older adults are inferior to younger ones. Even so, ageism still exists and will be discussed further in Myth #30, "Older adults hardly ever have trouble getting work." Although older adults may be at a disadvantage in jobs that emphasize speed and multitasking, they're highly capable of excelling in jobs that require care and accuracy as well as a store of knowledge and social skills.

## Older adults hardly ever have trouble getting work

Thanks to the Age Discrimination in Employment Act (ADEA), blatant instances of age discrimination are less common now than they were in the past. The ADEA was first enacted in the U.S. in 1967 and covered workers aged 40 to 65. It applied to companies with more than 20 employees and covered both the hiring and treatment of older workers. The ADEA was revised in 1978 to cover workers up to age 70. One further revision in 1986 eliminated, with some exceptions, any upper age limit for covered workers.

Since the enactment of the ADEA, job ads rarely state age requirements anymore, and job applications do not ask for age. Even so, when it comes to hiring, the ADEA laws are not easy to enforce – it's difficult to determine whether an older adult job applicant was as qualified as, or more qualified than, the younger applicant who was ultimately selected (Rix, 2011). The rare exception favoring older applicants seems to be for jobs considered stereotypically suitable for older adults. In one study (Perry, Kulik, & Bourhis, 1996), young adult business students expressed a positive attitude toward hiring older workers for jobs which at that time were considered well suited for older workers (selling stamps or coins), but they were less positive when the jobs were considered well suited for young workers (selling CDs). In some cases, older adults who are viewed as experts in a professional field may be in demand. For example, in the academic world it is not unusual for individuals in their 50s and even 60s to move to new colleges and universities for promotions or higher administrative positions. But for older individuals who are not established experts in select professions, being hired is not always easily accomplished, especially if they have lost their job in a recession and are trying to find a new one. In fact, older workers who lose their job are out of work longer than their younger counterparts, with an average duration of unemployment as long as 56 weeks as compared to 38.5 weeks for younger job-seekers (Rix, 2012).

The ADEA laws may be somewhat more effective when it comes to unfair treatment of older employees in the workplace. Employers cannot legally demote or terminate workers solely because of their age – rather, employers must show evidence that the older employee's work record is deficient, that the older employee's job has become obsolete, or that budgetary constraints necessitate letting an older employee go. Even so, the ADEA has not been successful in eradicating subtle forms of age discrimination such as denying older workers on-the-job opportunities or passing them over for promotions. But if older workers maintain careful records of their performance evaluations, those who think they have experienced age discrimination may be able to make a case for deserving something they did not get.

Nevertheless, in 2009, in the case of *Gross v. FBL Financial Services, Inc.*, the U.S. Supreme Court narrowed some of the protections of the ADEA . The court ruled that the standards of the Civil Rights Act of 1964 did not apply to the ADEA. This means that if age *is only one of several* reasons for firing or demoting an employee, then the employer is acting within the law. In contrast to the situation with other types of discrimination, age must be the *only* reason for discrimination for the employee to win an age-based claim. As a result of this Supreme Court decision, legislation (the Protecting Older Workers Against Discrimination in the Workplace Act) was introduced in the Senate in March of 2012 that would make it "clear that when a victim shows discrimination was a 'motivating factor' behind a decision, the burden is properly on the employer to show it complied with the law" (Senator Tom Harkin, 2012). Unfortunately, this law was not enacted (S. 2189, 2012). It failed at that time and was reintroduced on July 31, 2013 (Schuman, 2013, July 31). As of this writing, the 2009 Supreme Court decision holds: age discrimination is the only form of discrimination that has a special burden of proof; it must be the only reason for discrimination, rather than one of several reasons, in order for an employee to sue successfully.

The AARP (2012c) conducted a survey of 1,000 registered voters aged 50 and older to determine their attitudes toward age discrimination in the workplace and the then pending Protecting Older Workers Against Discrimination in the Workplace Act. Over one-third of those surveyed reported that they, or someone they knew, had in fact experienced age discrimination in the workplace. When they were provided a brief description of the 2009 Supreme Court case which makes it more difficult for older workers to make discrimination claims against employers, 81% of those surveyed believed it was important for Congress to take action to protect older workers.

In sum, the existence of the ADEA may be the reason for the myth that there is no age discrimination in the workplace. But age discrimination in hiring is difficult to monitor, and the fact is that older adults who lose their jobs are out of work for longer than are younger workers. Furthermore, the large number of age discrimination cases filed (though not necessarily won) by older plaintiffs, as well as the fact that many older adults think they or someone they know of have experienced age discrimination, testifies to the likelihood that many older workers are not leaving their jobs just because they want to (Sterns & Sterns, 1997).

## Retirement is depressing, so older adults only retire when they are forced to do so

For most adults, work is an essential part of life. Until recently, this may have been more so for men than for women, because men were more likely to spend decades of uninterrupted participation in the workforce. It stands to reason that giving up the work role abruptly calls for some degree of adjustment. The opening scene in the movie *About Schmidt*, a 2002 comedy drama based on a 1996 novel, shows a large wall clock with a second hand moving to 5 p.m. on actor Jack Nicholson's last day of work. This scene is capped by a formal but dreary retirement dinner, a scenario sure to reinforce the myth that retirement is not a desirable event. But is retirement actually a traumatic event, and do older adults really suffer from depression when they retire?

Prior to the enactment of the Age Discrimination in Employment Act (ADEA) in 1967, mandatory retirement was the rule for most jobs – workers had to retire at a specific age, typically 65. In 1986, the ADEA was amended to cover workers with no upper age limit. The result was that mandatory retirement was eliminated for most workers. If older adults were anxious to keep working beyond the age of 65, it would have been reasonable to predict that once the ADEA was implemented, the median age of retirement would increase. Yet the median age of retirement dropped from approximately 67 in 1950–1955 to approximately 63 in 1985–1990 (Gendell & Siegel, 1996), indicating a trend for workers to leave the paid labor force at a younger age.

Admittedly, many factors influenced the decline in retirement age, an important one being the prevalence in those years of Defined Benefit (DB) retirement plans. DB plans typically pay retired workers a pension (often in the form of a monthly check) for the rest of their lives if they have worked for a company or institution for the required length of time. Workers often plan to retire as soon as they qualify for a pension from their employer and/or when they are eligible for early (though reduced) Social Security benefits at age 62.

So what about the percentage of older adults who are still working? In 1985, 15.8% of Americans aged 65 and older were in the paid labor force. By 2012, 18.5% of adults aged 65 were in the paid labor force (U.S. Department of Health and Human Services, Administration on Aging, Administration for Community Living, 2012). The increase from 15.8% in 1985 to 18.5% in 2012 demonstrates the reality that Americans are continuing to work to later ages.

What factors might lead to older workers' increased labor force participation? Recent years have seen a drastic decline in the number of employers offering DB retirement plans that guarantee a pension check for the life of the retiree. If anything, the retirement plans available to most workers are of the Defined Contribution (DC) variety, wherein both the employee and the employer make regular contributions that are invested and grow tax-free. With the recession that hit in 2008, pension plan investments lost value, thus causing the worth of most DC retirement plans to shrink. This meant that the pool of money which older retirees could count on once they left the paid labor force was considerably reduced. The overall effect of this downturn has been that many older workers are postponing retirement, because if they continue to work they are able to build their retirement investments back up. Also, more years of work mean fewer years in retirement during which retirement investments will have to be expended. In sum, economic factors are a likely reason that older adults are now remaining in the workforce for longer.

In earlier times, many companies offered workshops for employees approaching age 65 that encouraged them to develop hobbies or interests that would fill the void once they retired. In contrast, much of today's advice to individuals who are about to retire involves money management. (Financial factors are discussed in more detail in Myth #32.) Aside from monetary factors, however, the myth that retirement is depressing likely has its roots in the belief that separation from the work role is a traumatic event with negative emotional implications, because work plays such a prime role in the identity of many people.

An ideal way to study the emotional effects of retirement would be to follow the same people from the years prior to retirement to those following it. This type of research is not easy to accomplish, but Reitzes, Mutran, and Fernandez (1998) conducted a two-year longitudinal study, testing levels of self-esteem and depression in 757 male and female workers (83% European American, ranging in age from 58 to 64) every six months. During the course of the study, 299 workers made the transition to retirement but the rest continued to work full-time. For both groups, the level of self-esteem remained relatively stable over time. Also, counter to the myth that retirement is depressing, depression scores actually declined in the group that retired. Perhaps the retired individuals enjoyed some relief from work-related stress.

Although it may appear so, retirement is not a sudden event for many people. Based on over 5,000 responses of men and women aged 51 to 61 who participated in the 1992 Health and Retirement Survey, Ekerdt, DeViney, and Kosloski (1996) found that the older respondents in the sample were more likely than the younger ones to have retirement plans. Also the men (especially those who were married) were more likely than the women to have concrete plans as well as an actual target date for retirement.

According to Atchley (1994), there can be a lengthy remote pre-retirement phase, during which workers entertain fantasies and ideas about what they wish to do in retirement. This phase is followed by a more immediate pre-retirement phase, during which concrete plans are laid. The actual event of separation from the labor force may be followed by a honeymoon phase, during which new retirees travel or engage in other activities that they could not do while employed. After some time spent in the honeymoon phase, retirees may experience a degree of emotional letdown (disenchantment phase). However, most retirees then go through a reorientation phase, during which they make efforts to establish a stable day-to-day life in retirement. Trips and special activities may still be on the agenda, but the pace is less frenetic. Atchley contends that not everyone goes through every single retirement phase in sequence, but in general, retirement is a process that occurs over time.

Many older adults look forward to retirement after years of hard work. This is more likely the case for those who anticipate an adequate income once they retire. It's particularly applicable to men who have worked consistently and know that they will receive a comfortable pension and/or have been able to accumulate adequate savings. Older men who are married, especially if they have a high level of marital satisfaction, are the most likely group to have a planned retirement date (Reitzes, Mutran, & Fernandez, 1998). Women are less likely to have a concrete target retirement date, possibly because their work history is less consistent – they do not qualify for a pension, their pension will not be adequate once they exit the workplace, and/or they have not been able to build an adequate nest egg.

So what do people do once they retire? Do retirees spend the day lying in a hammock sipping an ice-cold drink? Some retirees strive for continuity; for example, professionals such as teachers, lawyers, and physicians often continue to identify with their professions even if they are not actively practicing them on a full-time or even a part-time basis.

Nowadays, however, many older adults who retired from full-time careers may be working at *encore* careers. A 2011 Metlife Foundation/ Civic Ventures survey (combined telephone and online) of over 2,300 Americans aged 44 to 70 focused on the subject of encore careers. The authors of the survey posit that the way many people feel about their work changes after midlife, and they may be in search of a new kind of work that has deeper meaning than their first career. They want to focus on careers that provide purpose and passion but also a paycheck. Nearly a third of those surveyed viewed this next stage in their lives as a time to help others, but some saw it as a time to work just enough to cover expenses and maintain health insurance. Survey respondents who were currently in encore careers or interested in pursuing encore careers planned to work until an average age of 69.1 years and 68.6 years, respectively – 3.5 years longer than they had anticipated working a mere three years earlier. The majority (70%) of those pursuing an encore career wanted a personal stake in leaving the world better for future generations.

Retirees who do not work in paid jobs any longer often claim to be busier in retirement than they were when they were gainfully employed (Ekerdt, 1986). A sizeable proportion of older adults do volunteer work. Many retirees help out with grandchildren because their adult children have full-time jobs. For example, they pick up their grandchildren from school and care for them until the parents get home from work. Or they take care of grandchildren when schools are closed for vacation. Sadly, an increasing number of older retirees are actually raising grandchildren because of their own adult children's divorce, addiction, and so on (Hayslip & Kaminski, 2005). However, in a recent article in the *New York Times*, Korkki (2013, May 14) reports that some retirees opt to adopt children, some of whom are older or have special needs. Perhaps these retirees always wanted children but never had them, or they want to refill an empty nest now that they have the time and resources to enjoy doing so.

When contemplating what kind of life people will forge for themselves in retirement, we can revisit McCrae and Costa's (1987) Five-Factor Model of personality (NEO-AC: see Table 3.1), which we introduced in our discussion of Myth #17, "Older people are hypochondriacs." According to this model, there is stability across the adult years on five factors of personality and the traits subsumed under each. For example, individuals high on the neuroticism (N) factor are more likely to experience anxiety and related difficulties both before and after retirement compared to those low on this factor. Those high on the extraversion (E) factor likely had jobs that involved interacting with people. Once retired, they will probably become involved in social activities and/or volunteer work that can satisfy the same needs.

Before leaving our discussion of this myth, we should keep in mind that there will always be individuals who love to work and do not want to retire. They like the structure of getting up each day and going to a job. Perhaps the job offers a social network they don't want to give up. If they can't work full time, they may find *bridge* jobs, which usually involve part-time employment, either in an occupation similar to what they had before or perhaps in an entirely new occupation. Bridge employment allows a gradual transition from full-time employment to retirement (Bowen et al., 2011). Also, bridge jobs allow people to supplement their Social Security checks before they give up paid work altogether. As noted earlier, some older adults launch encore careers, working in a different field from the one in which they had earlier spent years or decades. Others might want to retire but financially cannot afford to, so they must continue to work.

In sum, the evidence does not support the myth that retirement is depressing or that people only retire when they are forced to do so. Individuals who plan for retirement ahead of time, who are in reasonably good health, and who have adequate finances usually look forward to and enjoy retirement. Nevertheless, for people who are forced to retire due to poor health or perhaps because of downsizing, retirement is not voluntary and could well be associated with negative outcomes, both physically and psychologically.

## Retired older adults are privileged financially

Myth 32

According to a Pew Research Center survey (2009), when asked to envision their lives after age 65, 67% of Americans (aged 18 to 64) anticipate that they will have more financial security than they do at present. The myth that older Americans are well-off may stem partly from the fact that they have "entitlements." Another aspect of this myth is that retired older adults are in an improved financial position because they have fewer expenses than they did when they were younger and still working. For example, their dry cleaning bills are down and they save on fast food because they have time to cook.

Thanks in part to Social Security (enacted in 1935) and Medicare (enacted in 1965), older adults as a group do enjoy a better standard of living today compared to earlier times. Those who reach a certain age and have worked for the required amount of time are eligible for Social Security benefit checks for the rest of their lives (an entitlement that younger generations fear will not be available to them). Originally, the age required for the full Social Security benefits was 65, but a Social Security Amendment passed in 1983 gradually raised the age of eligibility for full retirement benefits starting with people born after 1938. With this amendment, the age of eligibility for full benefits reached 66 for people born between 1943 and 1954. For people born after 1959, the age for full benefits will be 67. These increases in age of eligibility for full benefits addressed a growing concern about a possible shortage of funds and also took into account the improved health and longer average life expectancy of older Americans. The debate about whether to increase the age yet again is ongoing at the time of this writing.

There's little doubt that Social Security is an important factor in the decline in poverty rate among older adults, which was 35% in 1959 but only 8.7% by 2011. However, an additional 2.4 million, or 5.8% of the elderly, were classified as "near-poor," meaning that their incomes were less than 125% of the poverty level (U.S. Department of Health and Human Services, Administration on Aging, Administration for Community Living, 2012).

Social Security was never intended to replace 100% of working income. Rather, it was meant to serve as a financial cushion – a base level of economic security – for retired older Americans. Even so, as of 2010, 86% of older adults reported that Social Security was their major source of income (U.S. Department of Health and Human Services, Administration on Aging, Administration for Community Living, 2012).

In 2011, the median income for older Americans was $19,929–$27,707 for men and $15,362 for women (U.S. Department of Health and Human Services, Administration on Aging, Administration for Community Living, 2012). Living arrangements are an important factor when it comes to poverty, and older persons living alone were more likely to be poor (16.5%) than older persons living with families (5%). With regard to gender, 36% of women aged 65+ live alone, but only 19% of older men live alone; 72% of men live with a spouse, but only 46% of women live with one (U.S. Department of Health and Human Services, Administration on Aging, Administration for Community Living, 2012). So it should not be surprising that older women had a higher poverty rate (10.7%) than older men (6.2%).

Medicare is another entitlement available to individuals once they reach age 65. While working, employees pay a Medicare tax as well as a Social Security tax. When they reach age 65 they qualify for Medicare health insurance if they have worked and paid the Medicare tax for the required amount of time. Medicare Part A is free and covers many hospitalization costs, brief stays in a skilled nursing home, and short-term home health care following a hospital stay. Medicare Part B covers approximately 80% of health costs such as physicians' fees, laboratory tests, physical therapy, and some medical equipment. Medicare Part B is not free – the premiums are based on the older adults' income from all sources, even including earnings from tax-free municipal bonds.

Medicare has been under the gun lately, but it is an important reason for today's lower rate of poverty among older adults. However, it is important to keep in mind that Medicare Part B does have deductibles and co-payments even for covered services. For this reason, older adults who retire and are no longer covered under employer-sponsored health insurance usually purchase medi-gap insurance from private insurance companies so they will be fully covered for expenses not covered by Medicare Part B. Such policies can be costly and may not be affordable for all older retirees.

Some people mistakenly assume that Medicare will cover the expense of assisted living facilities and nursing homes if there comes a time when older adults need it. In reality, Medicare may cover brief nursing home stays following hospitalization, but it does not cover the cost of assisted living facilities or long stays in nursing homes. Long-term care insurance is often recommended to cover such costs. However, this type of insurance is costly (it can run into thousands of dollars a year), especially if purchased late in life, so it may be out of reach for many older Americans.

Given the high cost of assisted living and long-term stays in nursing homes, those who have not purchased long-term care insurance but now need these services are typically forced to "spend down" to deplete their savings so they can qualify for Medicaid. The reason for this is that Medicaid is a means-tested government program (meaning that to qualify for coverage, individuals must fall below a certain income level and can have only limited savings and personal property) that will cover medical expenses and long-term stays in nursing homes. Some people think older adults give money and property away to family members so they can qualify for Medicaid and thus be covered for long-term stays in nursing homes. Nevertheless, individuals, including family members, who have accepted monetary gifts from older adult Medicaid applicants within the past five years will be asked to return them.

In addition to the health-related expenses already mentioned, the cost of prescription (and possibly nonprescription) medications increases as people get older. The relatively recent Medicare Part D plan covers certain costs of prescription drugs but these are by no means free. The Medicare Part D premium varies depending on the specific plan an older adult selects. With Medicare Part D, not all medications are covered and there are co-payments for medications that are covered. Also, dental costs are not covered by Medicare or medi-gap policies, and the dental insurance policies available to retirees are usually expensive and very limited in coverage.

Overall, Social Security and Medicare have been successful in reducing the poverty rate among the older population, but do they free older adults from financial worries? To maintain a lifestyle close to what they had before retirement, older adults will need income in addition to Social Security. Also, if older adults do not want to incur medical expenses beyond what they can afford, they will need to purchase health insurance in addition to Medicare.

What about the assumption that the income people need once they retire is far less than what they required during their working years? It is true that items such as clothing and commuting costs will probably decline in retirement. Nevertheless, the total income people need in their retirement years is unlikely to decrease; in fact, it will probably increase. The most obvious reason for this increase is the cost of health care, as mentioned above. Health insurance costs increase for older adults who had subsidized insurance from an employer while they were still working. In some instances, retired employees may be able to keep their employer's health insurance, but usually they have to pay much more for it once they leave full-time employment.

Another item that increases in retirement is discretionary spending for things such as travel, hobbies, gifts, and entertainment. During their full-time work careers, many older adults dreamed of a life with sufficient income for these items, which may fall into the nonessential category but definitely add to the allure of having more leisure time. It may come as an unpleasant surprise to older retirees when they learn that the budget for such items will have to be severely curtailed so that they can afford essential expenses for food, housing, utilities, medical care, and taxes.

If older adults want to maintain a standard of living close to what they had while working, they will need a nest egg of savings that is sufficient to last throughout the years of retirement. There are many financial ideas on how best to ensure that retired individuals do not outlive their savings (see e.g. Quinn, 2013). Unfortunately, projections based on available figures for individuals approaching retirement indicate that the majority have nowhere close to the savings they will need even for the near-term, let alone for the decades that lie ahead.

Many older adults who retire were counting on their homestead to provide the nest egg they would need to supplement their Social Security benefits. Perhaps they planned to downsize from a large home to a smaller one, thus realizing extra cash to generate additional income once they left the workforce. Unfortunately, many locales have seen a decline in the value of the large homes that many retirees were counting on for extra income, and it may be difficult or impossible to sell those homes. Nevertheless, if older adults did not use their home equity as a piggy bank during the "go-go" years, they may be able to keep living in the same home without a mortgage, assuming they can afford the upkeep, and also provided that the home continues to provide a safe environment for them in their later years. It can be helpful that some states and counties make property tax allowances for retirees. Assuming housing prices recover (and they are already doing so in some areas), future retirees may be in a better position to use their homes as a nest egg, but this source of savings is no longer the safe haven it once was.

Related to the present discussion is a myth touched upon elsewhere (Myth #18) – that older adults are stingy and viewed as "greedy geezers." As we mentioned earlier, but it bears repeating here, many older adults provide financial help to adult children and grandchildren. Indeed, many older adults provide not only monetary help, but also housing and other types of support for adult children who have their lost jobs but have not found new ones that pay enough for them to adequately support their households. In fact, there is often more support going from the older to the younger generation than in the opposite direction (Fingerman & Birditt, 2011). This situation often continues until very late older adulthood, at which point people may begin to have health problems that affect how much support they are able to provide for the younger generation.

In sum, older adults who have worked for a sufficient amount of time are usually eligible for entitlements such as Social Security and Medicare. These entitlements provide a financial cushion, but they don't ensure a comfortable or carefree retirement. Given the economic turmoil of recent years, it's not surprising that we now hear much less about the importance of developing hobbies prior to retirement. Rather, we hear more about strategies for accumulating savings during the working years and preserving them once we retire so that we can approximate our pre-retirement lifestyle, or at the minimum just stay financially afloat.

# After they retire, older folks want to move to where it's warm

A prevalent myth is that just as soon as they retire, older adults head in droves to warmer climates where they live out their days in the sun. Fueling this myth is visible evidence for the construction of numerous retirement communities and condominiums in states such as Florida, Arizona, and North Carolina. In many areas, new communities with multiple senior living units and developments have created an economic boom because the expanding population of older retirees calls for shops, car dealerships, and all the other services necessary to support everyday living.

It is certainly the case that some retirees migrate to warmer climates, and their numbers are sufficiently large that it may appear to casual observers that all older adults are making long-distance moves. In reality, only a small percentage of older adults move to new communities (regardless of climate) when they retire, and an even smaller percentage relocate across state lines. The majority of older adults "age in place," meaning that they continue to live in the same locale and often in the same house where they resided prior to retirement.

Stoller and Longino (2001) studied the migration patterns of older adults who relocate to the Sunbelt once they retire. They found that this type of long-distance migration typically occurs among the *young-old* (65–74) age group, when individuals (often married couples) are in relatively good health, have adequate financial resources, and are able to enjoy the amenities offered by retirement communities. However, Stoller and Longino also noted a trend among people in *old-old* (75–84) age group to migrate in the reverse direction – from the Sunbelt back to the Frost Belt. The reasons for this outmigration were that by their mid- to late 70s, many individuals had become widowed and were beginning to experience moderate physical and/or cognitive difficulties. They were moving back to their home states to be closer to family members, including adult children.

The Urban Land Institute has produced a report on where people over the age of 65 are living now and also where they are expected to be living in the foreseeable future (McIlwain, 2012). Rather than refer to the young-old and old-old, the report distinguishes among groups by cohort as follows: the Greatest Generation (born between 1901 and 1927), the Silent Generation (born between 1928 and 1945), and the Leading-Edge Boomers (born between 1946 and 1956). The report notes that the

Leading-Edge Boomers are unique in that they are in better health than earlier generations were. They are expected to be active and productive for many years into the future. Furthermore, as we have noted elsewhere, those who fall into the Leading-Edge Boomer category have recently experienced an economic crisis. They tend to have less money saved for retirement and greater debt than did people in earlier generations when they were that age. It is expected that Leading-Edge Boomers will have to work longer than earlier generations did. Thus, it may well take an extra decade before they are ready to retire and possibly move into housing communities designed for older adults. This report predicts that the recent recession will slow any existing migration to the South and West. The housing crisis has trapped those in the Leading-Edge Boomer generation in their suburban communities, where they are unable to sell their homes. As a result, some of these suburban areas are becoming naturally occurring retirement communities.

In sum, it has always been the case that a relatively small percentage of older retirees uproot themselves to move across state lines in order to settle in milder climates. With the recent economic recession, however, this percentage is expected to be even lower. Even so, in today's world, it's likely that their adult children may not remain in the area where they grew up. In some cases, older retirees relocate to geographical areas that are not necessarily warm, but where an adult child has made his or her home.

# 5 ENDINGS AND LOSS

## All the good ones are either gay, married, or dead

People often assume that older widows don't get married because there just aren't enough single men to go around who can still enjoy a date. It's true that there are more single women than men in the older age groups, but the women are not all circling those few like sharks in the water. Obviously, there are plenty of women who are widowed and not dating, and for lots of reasons. But what about the ones who are dating? We would be wrong to assume that all of those women are hearing wedding bells.

*Great Myths of Aging*, First Edition. Joan T. Erber and Lenore T. Szuchman.
© 2015 John Wiley & Sons, Inc. Published 2015 by John Wiley & Sons, Inc.

# If older widows date, it's to find a new husband

In 2012, widows accounted for 37% of women aged 65 and older (U.S. Department of Health and Human Services, Administration on Aging, Administration for Community Living, 2012). It's generally assumed that these older widows would like to remarry and that when they decide to start dating, it's with the intention of finding a new husband.

Even if some older widows are hoping to remarry and are dating for the sole purpose of finding a new spouse, there's a good bit of evidence that this is not as common as people often assume. Watson and Stelle (2011) interviewed 14 white, middle-class, heterosexual women (aged 64 to 77) who lived in central Texas and were dating. Although dating was considered a path to remarriage for some of them, most of these women considered going out on a date just an opportunity to have fun and companionship. They viewed dating as a way to enhance an already satisfying life, but without the commitment of marriage. They did not necessarily want to give up their lives as independent women. Even so, they wanted a place in a couples-oriented world that would involve dancing, dinner, and movies, and, yes, also sexual intimacy in some cases.

Dickson, Hughes, and Walker (2005) interviewed women of a similar demographic, but from a large city in the western U.S. Their findings were similar to those of Watson and Stelle (2011) in that the women in this study also reported that they enjoyed dating and needed men in their lives. Even so, many of them felt that the men wanted more from them than they were willing to give – that is, the men wanted to get married. The authors labeled one theme prevalent in the women's responses as "nurse and purse." This refers to the fact that these women believed that many of the older single men (widowers or otherwise) they met were looking for someone to take care of them, and some felt that the men were after their money. The women in this study didn't want to lose their autonomy because of the potential ill health of a partner. Furthermore, they were hesitant to merge their finances.

Davidson (2001) interviewed 25 British women and 26 British men aged 65 to 92, all of whom had been widowed for at least two years. The women were much less likely than the men to have even considered remarriage. In fact, none of the women were in an exclusive cross-gender romantic relationship at the time of study, although eight of the men were. Furthermore, only one of the women said she would like to get married again. Davidson noted that the women tended to see men as selfish and as needing a woman to be empathetic and caring. These women felt that men (even healthy men) needed to be "looked after," and they thought that they had had enough of that. The main reason that these widows gave for not wishing to remarry was that they didn't want to look after another man. In addition, they couldn't imagine ever being able to replace a lost spouse. Furthermore, the women were enjoying their freedom. In contrast, none of the men in Davidson's study mentioned not wishing to care for a woman as a reason for not having remarried. "The popular image of young men relinquishing their freedom on marriage seems to be reversed in later life: It is women who resist being dragged kicking and screaming up the aisle" (pp. 315–316).

Some long-term marriages do become caregiving relationships, most commonly with wives caring for husbands. Spousal caregiving is stressful, and it can lead to a sense of burden and even to various types of physical distress. When the recipient of care dies, leaving a widow to start a new kind of life, you can imagine how this could be a mixed blessing. Death of a spouse can be a relief if being married entails caregiving 24/7 for someone who no longer recognizes you, as might be the case when the spouse has Alzheimer's disease. Nevertheless, in some cases, a surviving spouse who has served in a caregiving role to her deceased husband for a long period of time before his death might benefit from the feeling that she had been useful and that she and her husband had become especially close in the husband's final months. Even so, it's reasonable to appreciate the point of view of a widow who doesn't want to risk replaying this role by becoming a nurse a second time around.

In recent years, online dating services have made it easier for older adults to meet people and also easier for researchers to study the motivations older people have for dating. AARP (2012a) conducted a survey of 1,000 single (divorced, separated, widowed, never-married) men and women over the age of 50 and found that 27% of people who were currently dating were using an online dating site. More women than men said they were using online dating to find friendship/companionship, whereas more men than women used it to find intimacy/sexual relations.

Banking on the potential for increased online dating for older people, AARP has started its own dating site (powered by howaboutwe.com), which encourages older people to decide quickly about whether to forge ahead with a possible new relationship. A member starts by posting a profile and finding a likely candidate to contact with an idea for a date ("How about we…"). No long emails back and forth, no deciding whether to meet only after getting to know one another online or by phone. Men and women can just go on a date and then make a decision about further dates (AARP, 2012b).

So what are older adults putting in their profiles on this and similar dating sites? McIntosh, Locker, Briley, Ryan, and Scott (2011) compared Internet dating profiles on match.com posted by young (aged 25–35) and older (aged 65+) men and women. They found that younger women posted profiles that specified a preference for men who were slightly older, but older women shifted toward a preference for younger partners. The older women may be restricting their dating pool, but their preference for slightly younger men makes sense in light of the fact that in the 65+ age group, there are four times as many widows as widowers (U.S. Department of Health and Human Services, Administration on Aging, Administration for Community Living, 2012). However, the older women's profiles indicating a preference for slightly younger men could also signal their concern about the "nurse and purse" problem that we mentioned earlier. With regard to the "nurse" aspect, older women do not want to become caregivers to older men; by preferring younger men they hope to avoid this role. With regard to the "purse" aspect, older women had a higher preferred income for their dates than did younger women, whereas there was no such difference between older and younger men. Older women don't want to be the economic mainstay for a new mate.

In sum, the best way to find a new spouse is probably to start dating. If older widows want to remarry, then we should find evidence for that in their motives for dating. As it happens, there's been considerable recent research on the phenomenon of older adult singles' desire to enter the dating world. Although many older women want to date, they are not all in the game to find a husband. A fair proportion of them want the companionship they get from a man, but they want to maintain their independence. And they certainly are cautious about assuming the role of "nurse and purse."

## And then you die...

We've come to the end. There's nothing left to think about but death. A lot of people assume that a typical place to wait for death is in the dreaded nursing home. Nursing homes have a lot of bad connotations: foul odors, boring food, nothing to do except watch TV. Most people don't want to live or die in a nursing home. Fortunately, most people don't live or die there. In this section we look closely at the odds of ending up in a nursing home. Furthermore, for those who do reside in nursing homes, daily life doesn't have to be so dreadful. After learning in the section on myths about the self that aging is not so depressing after all, it shouldn't be surprising that suicide is not a problem across the board for older people. Men over age 80 are at increased risk, but not women. So our mythbusting is more nuanced in this case. In our discussion of this myth we offer some clues as to why suicide might be more of a problem for older men than for older women, but readers may have some ideas of their own about this. Finally, we take on the fear of death and see who the real scaredy cats are.

## Myth #35 A majority of older adults end up in nursing homes and stay there till they die

Nursing homes, often known as skilled nursing facilities, are intended for people who need more care than they can typically get at home or even in an assisted living facility, but less care than they would get in a hospital. Services provided in nursing homes generally include not only room and board, but also nursing care, medication management, personal care (assistance with activities of daily living – ADLs – which include bathing, dressing, eating, toileting, and transferring from bed to chair), and social/ recreational activities. Some nursing homes feel a bit like hospitals, whereas others are more homelike, with more personal decoration and less of an institutional feel. For residents with cognitive problems, the environment is more restrictive, and access is controlled so that they won't wander outside.

Average nursing home costs in 2012 were $222 per day for a semi-private room – that's $81,030 annually (MetLife Mature Market Institute, 2012). Medicare will cover nursing home costs for a limited period of time following hospitalization. Medicaid will pay these costs on a longer-term basis but only when individuals can demonstrate that they fall below a certain income level and possess only limited assets. Some people purchase expensive long-term care insurance to protect their nest egg from being depleted by these costs.

Assisted living facilities (ALFs) are for those who need help with some ADLs but not round-the-clock nursing supervision. ALFs often have nurses on staff to manage medications and monitor health. Typically, assisted living communities provide housekeeping, laundry, recreation, two or more meals per day, security, transportation, as well as care and medication management and monitoring. Very often residents need more and more help with ADLs as time goes by, and there may be additional charges for help beyond a certain minimum. Monthly costs in 2012 averaged $3,486 for ALFs that provide a middle range of services (MetLife

Mature Market Institute, 2012). Medicare doesn't cover any of these costs, though Medicaid might for certain facilities and for people who qualify through means testing (i.e., fall below a certain income and have few assets).

On the face of it, nursing homes seem like a perfectly reasonable choice for those who need the care. Nevertheless, a lot of people fear living in a nursing home more than they fear death. In one survey (Prince Market Research, 2007), 13% of people aged 65 and older identified moving into a nursing home as their greatest fear – and only 3% said that death was what they feared most. Aging in place (staying at home in one's community) is what 89% of these individuals considered most desirable. What people fear they'll find in a nursing home compared to aging in place is the loss of control over their lives. Recall that in Myth #20, "Older adults prefer to be taken care of – they don't want a lot of responsibilities," we summarized a classic research study (Langer & Rodin, 1976) in which nursing home residents were found to do much better, physically and emotionally, if they were responsible for the care of a plant compared with those who had a similar plant cared for by someone else. Given that finding, imagine how it would feel to have a disability that requires a degree of support, but perhaps not as much support as a nursing home provides. It's possible that many people in this situation fear that placement in a long-term care facility will require them to accept a level of care that's greater than their level of perceived need – greater than would be required by their perceived level of decline. That fear could be what is most stressful and discouraging (Hill, 2005).

Do the majority of people aged 65 and older live in nursing homes? Absolutely not! In 2011, only 3.6% of people aged 65 and older lived in institutional settings. The percentage increases with age, but it never gets anywhere near a majority. It's 1% for people aged 65 to 74, 3% for people aged 75 to 84, and 11% for people aged 85 and older (U.S. Department of Health and Human Services, Administration on Aging, Administration for Community Living, 2012).

Even though at any given moment only a small percentage of the older adult population resides in a nursing home, patients often spend some time in a nursing home after a hospital stay and a fairly large group of older people die there – although not nearly a majority. The Centers for Disease Control and Prevention (CDC, 2008) reports that in 2005, the following percentages of deaths occurred in nursing homes/long-term care facilities: 13% of people aged 65 to 74, 24% of people aged 75 to 84, and 42% of people aged 85 and older. In a study of 1,817 nursing home residents who died between 1992 and 2006 (Kelly et al., 2010), the median length of stay in the nursing home before death was less than six months. However, the individual differences are pretty large. Shorter nursing home stays at the end of life tend to go along with greater access to paid and informal caregiver support. So being male, being married, and having a higher net worth are associated with increased opportunities for care in a person's home environment. Thus, social and demographic factors play a role in how long people stay in nursing homes at the end of life.

Obviously, not everyone who lands in a nursing home dies there. Some go there following a hospital stay for rehabilitation, but then they return home. A fair number of nursing home residents head to a hospital with an acute problem and die there. In fact, more people die in hospitals than in nursing homes: 43% of those aged 65 to 74, 40% of those aged 75 to 84, and 34% of those aged 85 and older (CDC, 2008).

Most people wish to die at home, and more and more people are able to do so. According to the CDC (2011), in 1989, one-sixth of Americans died at home; by 2007, that figure had gone up to one-quarter. Obviously, place of death is related to the care that's available in that location; in 2007, people under age 65 were more likely to die at home (30%) than those 65 and older (24%). However, these statistics vary by culture: non-Hispanic whites were less likely to die while hospitalized and more likely to die in nursing homes than Hispanic or non-Hispanic black, Native American, or Asian or Pacific Islanders, who were more likely to remain at home until they had a need for acute care in a hospital. In a study of a random sample of Medicare beneficiaries who died in 2000, 2005, and 2009, Teno and colleagues (2013) confirmed the CDC data that more persons aged 65 and older were dying at home as time went by.

That takes care of the population statistics on site of death. However, we still haven't gotten to the question of whether individuals are able to die where they wish to die. Fischer, Min, Cervantes, and Kutner (2013) found a low rate of correspondence between hospital patients' preferred and actual site of death. These researchers recruited patients in three hospitals in the Denver area, asking their preferred site of death and then followed up for five years. At the start, 75% stated that they would like to die at home, 10% in the hospital, and 6% in a nursing home. Of those who died during the follow-up period, only 37% died where they stated they would prefer to die.

With so many living in dread of landing in a nursing home, it's not surprising that new models of skilled care are being developed. One example is the "Eden alternative," which is a new way of conceptualizing nursing home care as envisioned by the physician-director of a nursing home, Dr. William Thomas (Hill, 2005). He calculated that the medical model wasn't the best model for nursing homes, which are called *homes*, after all. His Eden alternative homes resemble homes, not hospitals. In these facilities, residents aren't forced to accept a greater level of care than they need. The residents and the staff simulate a family-based relationship that emphasizes connectedness. Residents can volunteer in childcare centers if they're up to it, and thus have opportunities to give as well as receive care, and they can have plants and pets. In general, to the extent they are able, residents have a lifestyle more similar to a home environment than a hospital.

In summary, a majority of older people don't end up in nursing homes for extended periods of time and stay until they die. The odds of dying in a nursing home do increase with age, but they've decreased overall in recent years. The fact is, the majority of older people want to die as members of the larger community and not in a care facility. Nevertheless, as of now, the best hope for people who need a lot of care seems to be in the form of innovative residential facilities that feel more like homes and less like the feared nursing home.

## Suicide is more common among adolescents and young adults than it is among older adults

Suicide makes news when it becomes a problem for a particular group, such as returning service persons and gay youth. Suicide among very old men isn't part of our national conversation. Yet, these are actually the folks with the highest suicide rate. According to the CDC, the suicide rate in 2010 in the U.S. was 12.43 per 100,000 persons. The breakdown of this figure by age and sex appears in Table 5.1.

A quick glance at Table 5.1 shows that the suicide rate is higher for men than it is for women in all age groups. Moreover, there are gender differences when we look at the rate of suicide from the young to the older years. For women, the suicide rate increases slightly through middle age and then declines somewhat. The suicide trajectory is very different for men, whose rate actually reaches a peak in older adulthood (especially in the 80s). The gender difference grows with age, nearly doubling for men over time, but changing much less for women. For the 85 and older age group, the rate is over 14 times higher for men than it is for women.

What about the ratio of attempted suicides to completed suicides? Researchers have found evidence that older people are more likely than younger people to succeed in their suicide attempts. Moscicki et al. (1988) examined suicide attempts in a sample of nearly 20,000 adults aged 18

**Table 5.1**   Suicide injury death rates per 100,000, U.S. 2010

| Age group | Rate for men | Rate for women |
|-----------|--------------|----------------|
| 15–19 | 11.70 | 3.13 |
| 20–24 | 22.23 | 4.66 |
| 25–29 | 23.12 | 5.17 |
| 30–34 | 21.85 | 5.53 |
| 35–39 | 23.62 | 7.02 |
| 40–44 | 25.60 | 7.87 |
| 45–49 | 30.11 | 8.67 |
| 50–54 | 30.71 | 9.41 |
| 55–59 | 30.02 | 8.88 |
| 60–64 | 24.88 | 7.02 |
| 65–69 | 22.98 | 5.36 |
| 70–74 | 25.28 | 4.03 |
| 75–79 | 29.91 | 4.04 |
| 80–84 | 35.65 | 3.33 |
| 85+ | 47.33 | 3.27 |

Source: Centers for Disease Control and Prevention, National Center for Injury Prevention and Control. Web-based Injury Statistics Query and Reporting System (WISQARS) [online] (2013, July 3).

and older from five different U.S. cities. Respondents completed face-to-face interviews that included a question about whether they had ever attempted suicide. (Obviously, these attempts had not succeeded.) Moscicki et al. found that the lowest prevalence of attempts occurred in the over 65 age group. Yet the oldest people have the highest actual suicide rate. According to Kastenbaum (2006), suicide attempts are "successful" in 1 out of 25 attempts for younger adults, but 1 out of 4 people aged 65 and older who attempt suicide actually complete the act.

Why are suicidal behaviors more lethal among older adults? Conwell, Duberstein, and Caine (2002) note that older adults have less physical resilience (less likely to recover from a botched attempt), experience greater isolation (less likely to be rescued or to be given emotional support if there are warnings), and perhaps are more determined to die. Also, compared to younger age groups, older people are likely to use more violent, and also more effective, methods for committing suicide. For example, Cohen and Eisdorfer (2011) report that in the general population, 57% of suicides involve firearms, but in the older age group that figure rises to 70%.

Kaplan, Huguet, McFarland, and Mandle (2012) used CDC data from 2003 to 2007 on male suicide decedents aged 65 and older from 16 states. It's reasonable to focus on men – recall from the CDC statistics cited at the beginning of this section that the suicide rate for men is much higher than it is for women. In this data base, nearly 80% of the 4,000 men who committed suicide had used a firearm, and the use of firearms as a means to commit suicide increases with age. Those who did use firearms were mostly white, married, veterans, and residents of southern states. Also, firearms were the means used in 90% of suicides that occurred in rural areas, where the availability of firearms tends to be greater. It's probable that men consider firearms to be a masculine way to deal with adversity; it might not be considered masculine to fail at a suicide attempt, and using a gun does ensure against failure in most cases. According to Kaplan et al., those who used firearms, rather than other methods, were significantly less likely to have been diagnosed and/or treated for mental health problems previously or to have had a prior suicide attempt. However, 67.7% of firearm users had physical health problems.

What are the psychological risk factors for older adult suicide? According to Conwell, Van Orden, and Caine (2011), "establishing causation of a complex, multidetermined, rare and dire outcome such as suicide is a daunting task" (p. 452). Because failed attempts aren't very common among older adults, one has to look back after the death to evaluate what might have been going on in the person's life. This is called a *psychological autopsy*. Conwell and his colleagues examined all of the well-conducted studies based on this method. After summarizing the risk factors, they conclude that the most prominent antecedent of suicide in older adults is psychiatric illness, most often major depression, which is present in up to 97% of cases. Poor physical health and functional impairments are often present, but this is also true of many older adults who don't commit suicide. Nevertheless, the relative risk for suicide increases with the number of acute and chronic illnesses a person has. It's also important to consider the meaning that an illness has for an individual and the impact of the illness with regard to function, pain, and feelings of personal integrity and autonomy. In addition, stressful events often cluster before suicide attempts, but for older adults these events are usually different than they are for young adults. For young and middle-aged adults, typical stressors are problems with relationships, finances, employment, and the law. By contrast, for older people stressors are more likely to be physical illness and losses. Also, there's a high likelihood that community-living older suicide victims live alone, so it may be that social isolation and loneliness add to their stress.

In a study conducted in Spain, Miret and her colleagues (2010) focused on suicidal intent, which is defined as the seriousness or intensity of the wish to commit suicide. Suicidal intent can be measured by such indicators as planning the suicide, taking precautions against intervention, and lack of communication with others about one's emotional situation. These researchers found that the majority of suicide attempts have low or moderate intent, but high intent is a good predictor of "success." Just as Conwell and his colleagues found with psychological autopsies, Miret et al. note that people with high intent are likely to be single, divorced, or widowed; to have a psychiatric diagnosis, especially depression; and to have experienced recent stressful events. Not surprisingly, older people have higher intent than younger people.

Researchers at the University of Michigan argue that substance abuse disorder (especially alcohol abuse) is the second most common psychiatric disorder after depression to be associated with suicide in the older age group (Blow, Brockmann, & Barry, 2004). Older people are more sensitive to the effects of alcohol than are younger people because of an age-related decrease in the ratio between lean body mass and fat. Also, liver enzymes that metabolize alcohol become less efficient with age, and central nervous system sensitivity to drugs increases with age. Thus, Blow et al. contend that older people might have a problem after consuming fewer drinks than younger people would. Also, they claim that alcohol use and misuse are more prevalent among the suicidal than the nonsuicidal elderly. Too much drinking may well interact with depression, so older people with depression get even more depressed when they drink. That would mean that alcohol could tip an already depressed person into thinking about suicide.

Another factor that might influence someone with depression to yield to thoughts of suicide is the perception of being a burden to loved ones, regardless of whether or not the loved ones actually do feel burdened. Jahn, Cukrowicz, Linton, and Prabhu (2011) studied *perceived burdensomeness* in a sample of 106 adults aged 60 to 93 recruited from a community health center in Texas. They found that people who were depressed and who also believed themselves to be a burden to others were more likely to entertain thoughts of suicide than those who were depressed but did not also have the perception of burdensomeness.

In summary, to make a determination about the myth that suicide is not a problem in the older population requires that we consider gender. Older women don't seem to be more at risk than women of other ages. However, older men, especially those aged 80 and older, are at notably higher risk for suicide than are people in any other group. In general, for older adults, the warnings (failed suicide attempts) that would alert family or professionals in the community are often not present, and the methods used to complete the act are particularly lethal. As a society, we should be especially watchful of older people (especially men) who are depressed and alone, who have multiple impairments and multiple stressors, who use alcohol in excess, and who feel that they're a burden to other family members. If they have access to firearms, so much the worse. Finally, although we don't often get warnings from potential older suicide victims, we should take very seriously any that we do get.

## Older people have the greatest fear of death of any age group – they are the closest to it, so they should know

Given the sharply escalating rate of death in older groups, it seems reasonable to assume (and most people do) that older adults fear death because there's a good probability they'll face it in the near future. In 2010, the following were the death rates by age per 100,000 people: 206.2 deaths in the 25–34 age group, 339.9 deaths in the 35–44 age group, 815.7 deaths in the 45–54 age group, 1,727.5 deaths in the 55–64 age group, 3,868.5 deaths in the 65–74 age group, 9,869.5 deaths in the 75–84 age group, and 13,934.3 deaths in the 85 and older age group (Murphy, Xu, & Kochanek, 2013). But despite their closeness to death, older people don't fear it as much as one might think.

One way to measure fear of death is to ask people how they feel about the end of life. Karl Pillemer (2011) conducted in-depth interviews with 300 older adults from all walks of life and religious backgrounds. He refers to these individuals as *experts* because they were nominated by organizations or friends for being particularly wise. To learn about the experts' views on death, Pillemer posed the following question: "When people reach your age, they begin to realize that there are more years behind them than in front of them. What are your feelings about the end of life?" (p. 141). In their responses, Pillemer's experts did not express an overpowering fear of death, nor was there any evidence of denial that death would occur. One 90-year-old expert stated firmly that she wasn't afraid to die and had no worries about it, though she did admit that she had had such fears when she was younger. Another expert, aged 94, considered death to be a natural part of life and expressed no fear about it. Yet another expert, aged 87, stated that her fear of death changed as she aged: earlier, she had felt a great deal of anxiety about the idea of dying, but she no longer thought about it much – her main goal now was to do everything she could do in the time she had left. A 73-year-old expert survived a life-threatening illness in his late 50s but was diagnosed recently with an illness that is usually terminal within a short period of time. He claimed to have no fear and felt that a realistic outlook about the imminence of his death made facing it easier.

In summing up the experts' responses, Pillemer concluded they had little worry about death itself. But even though the experts were not fearful about death, they did emphasize the importance of planning so that those left behind would not be burdened with a load of work. For many, planning involved ensuring that their wills were valid and up to date as well as checking that their finances, personal papers, and possessions were in order. Several experts thought "tidying up" possessions was analogous to tying up the loose ends of their lives, and engaging in such end-of-life activities helped them accept the inevitable. Experts beyond the age of 70 expressed a desire to "seize the day" and thought worrying was a waste of whatever time they might have left. Several experts were determined to visit close friends even if it meant distant travel – some actually informed friends that they were choosing to visit them while they were alive, rather than attending their funerals later on. Even so, some of the experts considered funerals a way to celebrate the deceased person's life, hardly a negative view.

Pillemer's experts' views on death are echoed in a study conducted in England. Field (2000) interviewed 28 men and 26 women between the ages of 65 and 80 to determine the validity of the widespread belief that older adults fear death. Of the total sample, only one woman expressed clear fearfulness about death. Eighteen of the 28 men reported that they were not fearful, and an additional seven reported they were no longer fearful (but maybe had been at an earlier time). Of the 26 women, 13 reported they were not fearful and an additional seven were no longer fearful. If anything, rather than fear of death itself, these individuals were more concerned about process of dying, including the possibility of an extended period of pain prior to death. Some were concerned about the effect their death might have on a spouse and therefore hoped they would not die first, leaving a spouse or other family members alone.

Older people tend to be concerned about the place of death and the type of death they will experience more than they are about the fact of death. Lloyd-Williams, Kennedy, Sixsmith, and Sixsmith (2007) interviewed 40 men and women ranging in age from 80 to 89, all of whom lived alone in the community. These individuals were a subsample from a larger study conducted in the U.K. and were selected to be diverse in terms of gender and health but also cognitively able to respond to open-ended questions regarding end-of-life issues. The majority of these individuals felt they had been graced with long lives, and they acknowledged that death was inevitable. They didn't want to become a burden to others should they be afflicted with a long and debilitating illness, and they wanted to have some control over when their lives would end. Some had already made funeral plans and arrangements in order to spare their relatives from any responsibility after their death. Research participants aged 80 and older in the U.S. expressed similar views – their main worry wasn't death but rather how and when death would occur and whether the dying process would be a burden to family members (Gold, 2011).

Overall, then, older adults as a group don't fear death itself. But are there individual differences in this regard? Fry (2003) conducted a survey of 167 women and 121 men from one of three similar mid-sized cities in Alberta, CA. These were predominantly European American individuals ranging in age from 65 to 87. Approximately 164 lived independently in the community, and the rest lived in semi-supervised assisted living settings. Fry found that self-efficacy ratings were significant predictors of fear of death and dying – compared with people with low feelings of self-efficacy, those with high feelings of self-efficacy reported less fear. (Self-efficacy is the belief in one's ability to succeed in a given domain, for example academics or relationships.) Interestingly, the researchers found gender differences in self-efficacy associated with fear of death and dying. For women, strong feelings of self-efficacy in the interpersonal and emotional domains were associated with lower fear of death and dying. Specifically, women who felt they could manage relationships with family, friends, and acquaintances (interpersonal self-efficacy) and felt confident they could remain emotionally balanced during periods of stress (emotional self-efficacy) expressed less fear of death and dying. For men, strong feelings of self-efficacy in the instrumental, organizational, and physical domains were associated with lower fear of death and dying. Specifically, men who felt they could manage instrumental daily needs such as using the phone and arranging transportation, who felt capable of organizing their business and financial affairs, and who had strong convictions about their physical health expressed less fear of death and dying. For men, but more so for women, self-efficacy in the domain of spiritual health – that is, the ability to generate spiritually based faith and inner strength – was associated with lower fear of death and dying.

In addition to feelings of self-efficacy, what other variables could have a bearing on whether, and to what degree, older adults fear death? Several researchers have investigated the role of religious belief, level of education, ethnic background, and type and extent of social support with regard to fear of death (see e.g. Fortner, Neimeyer, & Rybarczyk, 2000; Neimeyer & Fortner, 2006; Wink & Scott, 2005). As yet, there are no definitive answers as to exactly what factors or combination thereof may buffer individuals against the fear of death, but clearly not all older adults are the same.

Cicirelli (2002) interviewed European American and African American adults over the age of 60 and found no differences in their fear of death. Nevertheless, older adults with more physical problems and those living in institutional settings such as nursing homes expressed higher anxiety about death compared with those in who were in better health and living in the community. Perhaps older adults who are dependent upon others feel less in control of their environment and therefore experience more anxiety about death.

Again, despite individual differences, older adults as a group don't express a strong fear of death. But how do they compare with other age groups in this regard? Young adults find it difficult to imagine there might not be a long future stretching out in front of them (Thorson & Powell, 2000). The low rate of death for this age group certainly bodes well for a lengthy future, so it stands to reason they don't think about, much less fear, death. In contrast, middle-aged adults express greater fear of death not only compared to younger adults, but also compared to older adults (Fortner et al., 2000; Kastenbaum, 1999). Why might this be the case when the rate of death is so much higher for older adults than it is for middle-aged adults? First, middle-aged adults have greater caretaking responsibilities than older adults do. They may still have dependent children and many are providing help to the older generation. Middle-aged adults may well be anxious about leaving family members to function on their own. Older adults usually have fewer caregiving responsibilities – their children are probably well along into adulthood and hopefully have fashioned independent lives and are able to fend for themselves. Also, older adults are less likely than middle-aged adults to be assisting with elderly parents – after all, they are now elderly themselves! So any fear of death stemming from concern about leaving behind those who depend on them is justifiably allayed in the older adult age group, whereas such concern is likely at its peak in the middle-aged group. Second, older adults have had more time than middle-aged adults to carry out whatever they planned to do in their lives. Their lesser fear of death may stem from awareness that the future does not hold as many possibilities as it did earlier in their lives. Finally, older adults may express less anxiety about death because they have experienced the death of friends and loved ones with increasing frequency with the passing of time. In some sense, they are socialized to the possibility of death. It is not uncommon for older adults to read the obituaries in local newspapers on a daily basis.

In sum, although older adults are closer to death than any other age group, they don't express much fear of death itself. There are individual differences of course, but in general, their concern lies more with the circumstances of dying – they wish to have some control over the dying process and to die with dignity.

# REFERENCES

AARP. (1999). *AARP*/Modern Maturity *sexuality study*. Retrieved April 18, 2014 from http://assets.aarp.org/rgcenter/health/mmsexsurvey.pdf

AARP. (2010). *Sex, romance, and relationships: AARP survey of midlife and older adults*. Retrieved April 18, 2014 from http://assets.aarp.org/rgcenter/general/srr_09.pdf

AARP. (2012a). AARP dives into the 50+ dating pool with launch of "AARP Dating" website powered by howaboutwe, new resources and content [Press release]. Retrieved April 21, 2014 from http://www.aarp.org/about-aarp/press-center/info-12-2012/AARP-dives-into-the-50-dating-pool-with-launch-of-AARP-dating-website-powered-by-howaboutwe-new-resources-and-content.html

AARP. (2012b). *AARP online dating survey*. Retrieved April 18, 2014 from http://www.aarp.org/content/dam/aarp/research/surveys_statistics/general/2012/AARP-Online-Dating-Survey-AARP.pdf

AARP. (2012c). *Protecting older workers against discrimination act: National public opinion report*. Retrieved April 18, 2014 from http://www.aarp.org/content/dam/aarp/research/surveys_statistics/work_and_retirement/powada-national.pdf

Abrahms, S. (2013, April). Three generations under one roof. *AARP Bulletin*, *54*(3), 16–20.

Adler, J. (2002, February 25). The "thrill" of theft. *Newsweek*, *139*(8), 52–53.

Adler, J. (2007, June 3). Raising buildings for grandparents who are raising kids. *Chicago Tribune*. Retrieved April 18, 2014 from http://articles.chicagotribune.com/2007-06-03/business/0706020267_1_apartment-building-seniors-grandparents-step

Age Discrimination in Employment Act of 1967, 29 U.S.C. 621 nt *et seq*. Retrieved April 18, 2014 from http://www.house.gov/legcoun/Comps/Age%20Discrimination%20In%20Employment%20Act%20Of%201967.pdf

Alzheimer's Association. (2013). *Know the 10 signs*. Retrieved April 18, 2014 from http://www.alz.org/co/in_my_community_alzheimers_symptoms.asp

Amariglio, R. E., Townsend, M. K., Grodstein, F., Sperling, R. A., & Rentz, D. M. (2011). Specific subjective memory complaints in older persons may indicate poor cognitive function. *Journal of the American Geriatrics Society*, *59*, 1612–1617. doi: 10.1111/j.1532-5415.2011.03543.x

American Cancer Society. (2013). *Breast cancer overview.* Retrieved April 18, 2014 from http://www.cancer.org/cancer/breastcancer/overviewguide/breast-cancer-overview-key-statistics

American Psychiatric Association. (2013). *Highlights of changes from DSM-IV-TR to DSM-5.* Retrieved April 18, 2014 from http://www.dsm5.org/Documents/changes%20from%20dsm-iv-tr%20to%20dsm-5.pdf

American Psychological Association. (2013). *Guidelines for psychological practice with older adults.* Retrieved April 18, 2014 from http://www.apa.org/practice/guidelines/older-adults.aspx

American Society for Aesthetic Plastic Surgery. (2012). *Cosmetic surgery national data bank statistics 2012.* Retrieved April 18, 2014 from http://www.surgery.org/sites/default/files/ASAPS-2012-Stats.pdf

Angell, R. (2014, February 17 & 24). This old man: Life in the nineties. *The New Yorker*, 60–65.

Ansley, J., & Erber, J. T. (1988). Computer interaction: Effect on attitude and performance in older adults. *Educational Gerontology*, *14*, 107–119.

Ardelt, M. (2000). Antecedents and effects of wisdom in old age. *Research on Aging*, *22*, 360–394.

Ardelt, M. (2011). Wisdom, age, and well-being. In K. W. Schaie & S. L. Willis (Eds.), *Handbook of the psychology of aging* (7th ed.) (pp. 279–291). San Diego: Elsevier Academic Press.

Atchley, R. C. (1994). *Social forces and aging* (7th ed.). Belmont, CA: Wadsworth.

Ayers, C. R., Sorrell, J. T., Thorp, S. R., & Wetherell, J. L. (2007). Evidence-based psychological treatments for late-life anxiety. *Psychology and Aging*, *22*, 8–17.

Bacon, C. G., Mittleman, M. A., Kawachi, I., Giovannucci, E., Glasser, D. B., & Rimm, E. B. (2003). Sexual function in men older than 50 years of age: Results from the Health Professionals Follow-up Study. *Annals of Internal Medicine*, *139*, 161–168.

Ball, K. K., Clay, O. J., Wadley, V. G., Roth, D. L., Edwards, J. D., & Roenker, D. L. (2005). Predicting driving performance in older adults with the useful field of view test: A meta-analysis. In University of Iowa, Public Policy Center (Ed.), *Proceedings of the 3rd International Driving Symposium on Human Factors in Driver Assessment, Training, and Vehicle Design.* (pp. 51–57). Iowa City: University of Iowa, Public Policy Center. Retrieved April 18, 2014 from http://drivingassessment.uiowa.edu/DA2005/PDF/08_KarleneBallformat.pdf

Baltes, P. B. (1993). The aging mind: Potential and limits. *The Gerontologist*, *33*, 580–594.

Baltes, P. B., & Schaie, K. W. (1974). Aging and IQ: The myth of the twilight years. *Psychology Today*, *7*, 35–40.

Baltes, P. B., & Schaie, K. W. (1976). On the plasticity of intelligence in adulthood and old age: Where Horn and Donaldson fail. *American Psychologist*, *31*, 720–725.

Baltes, P. B., & Staudinger, U. M. (1995). Wisdom. In G. L. Maddox (Ed.), *The encyclopedia of aging* (2nd ed.) (pp. 971–974). New York: Springer.

Barsky, A. J., Frank, C. B., Cleary, P. D., Wyshak, G., & Klerman G. L. (1991). The relation between hypochondriasis and age. *The American Journal of Psychiatry, 148,* 923–928.

Barsky, A. J., Wyshak, G., Klerman, G. L., & Latham, K. S. (1990). The prevalence of hypochondriasis in medical outpatients. *Social Psychiatry and Psychiatric Epidemiology, 25,* 89–94.

Bengston, V., Rosenthal, C., & Burton, L. (1996). Paradoxes of families and aging. In R. H. Binstock & L. K. George (Eds.), *Handbook of aging and the social sciences* (4th ed.) (pp. 253–282). San Diego: Academic Press.

Birditt, K. S., Fingerman, K. L., & Almeida, D. M. (2005). Age differences in exposure and reactions to interpersonal tensions: A daily diary study. *Psychology and Aging, 20,* 330–340.

Birren, J. E., & Fisher, L. M. (1990). The elements of wisdom: Overview and integration. In R. J. Sternberg (Ed.), *Wisdom: Its nature, origins, and development* (pp. 317–332). New York: Cambridge University Press.

Birren, J. E., & Schroots, J. J. F. (1996). History, concepts, and theory in the psychology of aging. In J. E. Birren & K. W. Schaie (Eds.), *Handbook of the psychology of aging* (4th ed.) (pp. 3–23). San Diego: Academic Press.

Block, J., Segal, R., & Segal, J. (2013). *Lewy Body Dementia: Signs, symptoms, treatment, caregiving, and support.* Retrieved April 18, 2014 from http://helpguide.org/elder/lewy_body_disease.htm

Blow, F. C., Brockmann, L. M., & Barry, K. L. (2004). Role of alcohol in late-life suicide. *Alcoholism: Clinical and Experimental Research, 28,* 48S–56S. doi: 10.1097/01.ALC.0000127414.15000.83?

Bohlmeijer, E. T., Westerhof, G. J., & Emmerik-de Jong, M. (2008). The effects of integrative reminiscence on meaning in life: Results of a quasi-experimental study. *Aging & Mental Health, 12,* 639–646. doi: 10.1080/13607860802343209

Boston, A. F., & Merrick, P. L. (2010). Health anxiety among older people: An exploratory study of health anxiety and safety behaviors in a cohort of older adults in New Zealand. *International Psychogeriatrics, 22,* 449–458. doi: 10.1017/S1041610209991712

Botwinick, J. (1984). *Aging and behavior* (3rd ed.). New York: Springer.

Bowen, C. E., Noack, M. G., & Staudinger, U. M. (2011). Aging in the work context. In K.W. Schaie & S. L. Willis (Eds.), *Handbook of the psychology of aging* (7th ed.) (pp. 263–277). San Diego: Elsevier Academic Press.

Braithwaite, V. A. (1986). Old age stereotypes: Reconciling contradictions. *Journal of Gerontology, 41,* 353–360.

Braitman, K. A., Kirley, B. B., Chaudhary, N. K., & Ferguson, S. A. (2007). Factors leading to older drivers' intersection crashes. *Traffic Injury Prevention, 8,* 267–274.

Braver, E. R., & Trempel, R. E. (2004). Are older drives actually at higher risk of involvement in collisions resulting in deaths or non-fatal injuries among their passengers and other road users? *Injury Prevention, 10,* 27–32. doi: 10.1136/ip.2003.002923

Brown, S. L., & Lin, I.-F. (2012). The gray divorce revolution: Rising divorce among middle-aged and older adults, 1990–2010. *Journals of Gerontology Series B: Psychological Sciences and Social Sciences, 67,* 731–741. doi:10.1093/geronb/gbs089.

Buss, D. M. (1989). Sex differences in human mate preferences: Evolutionary hypotheses tested in 37 cultures. *Behavioral and Brain Sciences, 12,* 1–49.

Butler, R. N., Lewis, M. I., & Sunderland, T. (1998). *Aging and mental health: Positive psychosocial and biomedical approaches* (5th ed.). Boston: Allyn & Bacon.

Cantor, M. (1979). Neighbors and friends: An overlooked resource in the informal support system. *Research on Aging, 1,* 434–463.

Carstensen, L. L. (1991). Socioemotional selectivity theory: Social activity in life-span context. In K. W. Schaie & M. P. Lawton (Eds.), *Annual review of gerontology and geriatrics* (Vol. 11, pp. 195–217). New York: Springer.

Carstensen, L. L. (1995). Evidence for a life-span theory of socioemotional selectivity. *Current Directions in Psychological Science, 4,* 151–156.

Carstensen, L. L., Gottman, J. M., & Levenson, R. W. (1995). Emotional behavior in long-term marriage. *Psychology and Aging, 10,* 140–149.

Carstensen, L. L., Gross, J. J., & Fung, H. H. (1997). The social context of emotional experience. In K. W. Schaie & M. P. Lawton (Eds.), *Annual review of gerontology and geriatrics* (Vol. 17, pp. 325–352). New York: Springer.

Castle, E., Eisenberger, N. I., Seeman, T. E., Moons, W. G., Boggero, I. A., Grinblatt, M. S., & Taylor, S. (2012). Neural and behavioral bases of age differences in perceptions of trust. *Proceedings of the National Academy of Sciences of the United States of America.* doi:10.1073/pnas.1218518109

CDC (Centers for Disease Control and Prevention). (2008). *Deaths by place of death, age, race, and sex: United States, 2005.* Worktable 309. Retrieved April 18, 2014 from http://www.cdc.gov/nchs/data/dvs/Mortfinal2005_worktable_309.pdf

CDC (Centers for Disease Control and Prevention). (2010). *Current depression among adults – United States, 2006 and 2008: Morbidity and Mortality Weekly Report, October 1, 2010, Erratum.* Retrieved April 18, 2014 from http://www.cdc.gov/features/dsdepression/revised_table_estimates_for_depression_mmwr_erratum_feb-2011.pdf

CDC (Centers for Disease Control and Prevention). (2011). *Health, United States, 2010: With special feature on death and dying.* Retrieved April 18, 2014 from http://www.cdc.gov/nchs/data/hus/hus10.pdf

CDC (Centers for Disease Control and Prevention). (2012). *Falls among older adults: An overview.* Retrieved April 18, 2014 from http://www.cdc.gov/homeandrecreationalsafety/falls/adultfalls.html

CDC (Centers for Disease Control and Prevention). (2013a). *National marriage and divorce rate trends,* Retrieved April 18, 2014 from http://www.cdc.gov/nchs/nvss/marriage_divorce_tables.htm

CDC (Centers for Disease Control and Prevention). (2013b). *Older adult drivers: Get the facts.* Retrieved April 18, 2014 from http://www.cdc.gov/Motorvehiclesafety/Older_Adult_Drivers/adult-drivers_factsheet.html

CDC (Centers for Disease Control and Prevention), National Center for Injury Prevention and Control. Web-based Injury Statistics Query and Reporting System (WISQARS) [online]. (2013, July 3) Retrieved April 18, 2014 from www.cdc.gov/ncipc/wisqars

Chan, W., McCrae, R. R., De Fruyt, F., Jussim, L., Löckenhoff, C. E., De Bolle, M. ..., &Terracciano, A. (2012). Stereotypes of age differences in personality traits: Universal and accurate? *Journal of Personality and Social Psychology, 103,* 1050–1066. doi: 10.1037/a0029712

Charles, S. T. (2011). Emotional experience and regulation in later life. In K. W. Schaie & S. L. Willis (Eds.), *Handbook of the psychology of aging* (7th ed.) (pp. 295–310). San Diego: Elsevier Academic Press.

Chen, J. (2012, November 11). What if grandpa doesn't really have Alzheimer's? *Parade Magazine, 22.*

Chen, Y., & Persson, A. (2002). Internet use among young and older adults: Relation to psychological well-being. *Educational Gerontology, 28,* 731–744. doi: 10.1037/a0029712

Chien, W., & Lin, F. R. (2012). Prevalence of hearing aid use among older adults in the United States. *Archives of Internal Medicine, 172,* 292–293. doi: 10.1001/archinternmed.2011.1408

Cicirelli, V. G. (1995). Siblings. In G. L. Maddox (Ed.), *The encyclopedia of aging* (2nd ed.) (pp. 857–859). New York: Springer.

Cicirelli, V. G. (2002). Fear of death in older adults: Predictions from terror management theory. *Journal of Gerontology: Psychological Sciences, 57B,* P358–P366. doi: 10.1093/geronb/57.4.P358

Cleveland, J. N., & Shore, L. M. (2007). Work and employment: Individual. In J. E. Birren (Ed.), *Encyclopedia of gerontology: Age, aging, and the aged* (2nd ed.) (Vol. 2, pp. 683–694). Boston: Elsevier Academic Press.

Cohen, D., & Eisdorfer, C. (2011). *Integrated textbook of geriatric mental health.* Baltimore: Johns Hopkins University Press.

Connidis, I. A. (1989). *Family ties and aging.* Toronto: Butterworths.

Connidis, I. A. (1994). Sibling support in older age. *Journal of Gerontology: Social Sciences, 49,* S309–S317.

Conwell, Y., Duberstein, P. R., & Caine, E. D. (2002). Risk factors for suicide in later life. *Biological Psychiatry, 52,* 193–204.

Conwell, Y., Van Orden, K., & Caine, E. D. (2011). Suicide in older adults. *Psychiatric Clinics of North America, 34,* 451–468. doi:10.1016/j.psc.2011.02.002

Corey-Bloom, J. (2000). Dementia. In S. K. Whitbourne (Ed.), *Psychopathology in later adulthood* (pp. 217–243). New York: John Wiley.

Costa, P. T., Jr., & McCrae, R. R. (1985). Hypochrondriasis, neuroticism, and aging: When are somatic complaints unfounded? *American Psychologist, 40,* 19–28.

Cross, S., & Markus, H. (1991). Possible selves across the life span. *Human Development, 32*, 230–255.

Cuddy, A. J. C., & Fiske, S. T. (2002). Doddering but dear: Process, content, and function of stereotyping older persons. In T. D. Nelson (Ed.), *Ageism: Stereotyping and prejudice against older persons* (pp. 3–26). Cambridge, MA: MIT Press.

Cuddy, A. J. C., Norton, M. I., & Fiske, S. T. (2005). This old stereotype: The pervasiveness and persistence of the elderly stereotype. *Journal of Social Issues, 61*, 267–285. doi: 10.1111/j.1540-4560.2005.00405.x

Cuijpers, P., van Straten, A., Smit, F., & Andersson, G. (2009). Is psychotherapy for depression equally effective in younger and older adults? A meta-regression analysis. *International Psychogeriatrics, 21*, 16–24. doi: 10.1017/S1041610208008089

Cullers, R. (2012, November 28). Vaginal lubricant uses slippery marketing tactic of female empowerment: Canadian ads for Mae by Damiva. *Adweek.* Retrieved April 18, 2014 from www.adweek.com/adfreak/vaginal-lubricant-uses-slippery-marketing-tactic-female-empowerment-145478

Cumming, E. M., & Henry, W. (1961). *Growing old: The process of disengagement.* New York: Basic Books.

Czaja, S. J. (2001). Technological change and the older worker. In J. E. Birren and K. W. Schaie (Eds.), *Handbook of the psychology of aging* (5th ed.) (pp. 547–568). San Diego: Academic Press.

Czaja, S. J., & Sharit, J. (1993). Age differences in the performance of computer based work as a function of pacing and task complexity. *Psychology and Aging, 8*, 59–67.

Davidson, K. (2001). Late life widowhood, selfishness and new partnership choices: A gendered perspective. *Ageing and Society, 21*, 297–317. doi:10.1017/S0144686X01008169

DeAngelis, T. (2009, November). In the driver's seat. *Monitor on Psychology.* Retrieved April 18, 2014 from the American Psychological Association website: http://www.apa.org/monitor/2009/11/drive.aspx

DeLamater, J. (2012). Sexual expression in later life: A review and synthesis. *Journal of Sex Research, 49*, 125–141. doi: 10.1080/00224499.2011.603168

Delbaere, D., Crombez, G., Van Den Noortgate, N., Willems, T., & Cambier, D. (2006). The risk of being fearful or fearless of falls in older people: An empirical validation. *Disability and Rehabilitation, 28*, 751–756. doi: 10.1080/09638280500304794

DePaulo, B. M., & Morris, W. L. (2006). The unrecognized stereotyping and discrimination against singles. *Current Directions in Psychological Science, 15*, 251–254. doi: 10.1111/j.1467-8721.2006.00446.x

Dickson, F. C., Hughes, P. C., & Walker, K. L. (2005). An exploratory investigation into dating among later-life women. *Western Journal of Communication, 69*, 67–82. doi: 10.1080/10570310500034196

Duggan, M., & Rainie, L. (2012). *Cell phone activities 2012.* Pew Research Center's Internet & American Life Project. Retrieved June 17, 2014, from http://pewinternet.org/~/media//Files/Reports/2012/PIP_CellActivities_11.25.pdf

Eaton, A., Visser, P. S., Krosnick, J. A., & Anand, S. (2009). Social power and attitude strength over the life course. *Personality and Social Psychology Bulletin, 35*, 1646–1660. doi: 10.1177/0146167209349114

Ekerdt, D. J. (1986). The busy ethic: Moral continuity between work and retirement. *Gerontologist, 26*, 239–244.

Ekerdt, D. J., & DeViney, S. (1993). Evidence for a preretirement process among older male workers. *Journal of Gerontology: Social Sciences, 48*, S35–S43.

Ekerdt, D. J., DeViney, S., & Kosloski, K. (1996). Profiling plans for retirement. *Journal of Gerontology: Social Sciences, 51B*, S140–S149.

Elderhostel. (2010). *2010 Annual Report.* Retrieved April 18, 2014 from http://roadscholar.org/support/EH_AnnualReport_Feb11_NoDonors.pdf

Ellin, A. (2011, August 8). The golden years, polished with surgery. *New York Times.* Retrieved April 18, 2014 from http://www.nytimes.com/2011/08/09/health/09plastic.html?pagewanted=all&_r=0

Ellin, A. (2013, April 22). How therapy can help in the golden years. *New York Times.* Retrieved April 18, 2014 from http://well.blogs.nytimes.com/2013/04/22/how-therapy-can-help-in-the-golden-years/?_r=0

Erber, J. T. (2013). *Aging and older adulthood* (3rd ed). New York: Wiley.

Erber, J. T., Szuchman, L. T., & Prager, I. G. (2001). Ain't misbehavin': The effects of aging and intentionality on judgments about misconduct. *Psychology and Aging, 16*, 85–95.

Etcoff, N., Orbach, S., Scott, & D'Agostino, H. (2004). *The real truth about beauty: A global report.* White Paper commissioned by Dove. Retrieved April 18, 2014 from http://www.clubofamsterdam.com/contentarticles/52%20Beauty/dove_white_paper_final.pdf

Federal Bureau of Investigation. (n.d.). *Fraud target: Senior citizens.* Retrieved April 18, 2014 from http://www.fbi.gov/scams-safety/fraud/seniors

Festa, E. K., Ott, B. R., Manning, K. J., Davis, J. D., & Heindel, W. C. (2012). Effect of cognitive status on self-regulatory driving behavior in older adults: An assessment of naturalistic driving using in-car video recordings. *Journal of Geriatric Psychiatry and Neurology, 26*, 10–18. doi: 10.1177/0891988712473801

Field, D. (2000). Older people's attitudes towards death in England. *Mortality, 5*, 277–297.

Fingerman, K. L. (1998). The good, the bad, and the worrisome: Emotional complexities in grandparents' experiences with individual grandchildren. *Family Relations, 47*, 403–414.

Fingerman, K. L. (2004). The role of offspring and in-laws in grandparents' ties to their grandchildren. *Journal of Family Issues, 25*, 1026–1049. doi: 10.1177/0192513X04265941

Fingerman, K. L., & Birditt, K. S. (2011). Relationships between adults and their aging parents. In K. W. Schaie & S. L. Willis (Eds.), *Handbook of the psychology of aging* (7th ed.) (pp 219–232). San Diego: Elsevier Academic Press.

Fischer, S., Min, S. J., Cervantes, L., & Kutner, J. (2013). Where do you want to spend your last days of life? Low concordance between preferred and actual site of death among hospitalized adults. *Journal of Hospital Medicine, 8*, 178–183. doi: 10.1002/jhm.2018

Fortner, B. V., Neimeyer, R. A., & Rybarczyk, B. (2000). Correlates of death anxiety in older adults: A comprehensive review. In A. Tomer (Ed.), *Death attitudes and the older adult: Theories, concepts, and applications* (pp. 95–108). Philadelphia: Brunner-Routledge.

Fredrickson, B. L., & Carstensen, L. L. (1990). Choosing social partners: How old age and anticipated endings make us more selective. *Psychology and Aging, 5*, 335–357.

Fry, P. S. (2003). Perceived self-efficacy domains as predictors of fear of the unknown and fear of dying among older adults. *Psychology and Aging, 18*, 274–286.

Fung, H. H., Carstensen, L. L., & Lutz, A. (1999). The influence of time on social preferences: Implications for life-span development. *Psychology and Aging, 14*, 595–604.

Gatz, M. (2007). Genetics, dementia, and the elderly. *Current Directions in Psychological Science, 16*, 123–127. doi: 10.1111/j.1467-8721.2007.00488.x

Gatz, M., Kasl-Godley, J. E., & Karel, J. J. (1996). Aging and mental disorders. In J. E. Birren & K. W. Schaie (Eds.), *Handbook of the psychology of aging* (4th ed.) (pp. 365–382). San Diego: Academic Press.

Gendell, M., & Siegel, J. S. (1996). Trends in retirement age in the United States, 1955–1993, by sex and race. *Journal of Gerontology: Social Sciences, 51B*, S132–S139.

Giarrusso, R., & Silverstein, M. (1995). Grandparent–grandchild relationships. In G. L. Maddox (Ed.), *The encyclopedia of aging* (2nd ed.) (pp. 421–422). New York: Springer.

Glück, J., & Bluck, S. (2011). Lay people's conceptions of wisdom and its development: Cognitive and integrative views. *The Journals of Gerontology, Series B: Psychological Sciences and Social Sciences, 66*, 321–324.

Gold, D. T. (1989). Sibling relationships in old age: A typology. *International Journal of Aging and Human Development, 28*, 37–51.

Gold, D. T. (1990). Late-life sibling relationships: Does race affect typological distribution? *Gerontologist, 30*, 741–748.

Gold, D. T. (2011). Late-life death and dying in 21st-century America. In R. H. Binstock & L. K. George (Eds.), *Handbook of aging and the social sciences* (7th ed.) (pp 235–247). San Diego: Elsevier Academic Press.

*Gross v. FBL Financial Services, Inc.,* 129 S. Ct. 2343 (2009). Retrieved April 18, 2014 from http://scholar.google.com/scholar_case?case=11161861274984420 877&hl=en&as_sdt=2&as_vis=1&oi=scholarr

Gross, J. J., Carstensen, L. L., Pasupathi, M., Tsai, J., Skorpen, C. G., & Hsu, A. Y. (1997). Emotion and aging: Experience, expression, and control. *Psychology and Aging, 12*, 590–599.

Gruenewald, T. L., Karlamangla, A. S., Greendale, G. A., Singer, B. H., & Seeman, T. E. (2007). Feelings of usefulness to others as a predictor of disability and mortality in older adults: The MacArthur Study of Successful Aging. *Journals of Gerontology: Psychological Sciences*, *62B*, P28–P37.

Gruley, B. (2013, July 22). Boomer sex with dementia foreshadowed in nursing home. Retrieved April 18, 2014 from http://www.bloomberg.com/news/2013-07-22/boomer-sex-with-dementia-foreshadowed-in-nursing-home.html

Haight, B. K., Michel, Y., & Hendrix, S. (1998). Life review: Preventing despair in newly relocated nursing home residents: Short- and long-term effects. *International Journal of Aging and Human Development*, *47*, 119–143.

Hamid, E., & Victor, D. (2014, February 13). When New Yorkers use umbrellas during snowstorms. [*City Room*] [Web log] Retrieved April 18, 2014 from http://cityroom.blogs.nytimes.com/2014/02/13/when-new-yorkers-use-umbrellas-during-snowstorms/

Hamilton, H. (2013). *Listen up to smarter, smaller hearing aids*. Retrieved April 18, 2014 from http://www.npr.org/blogs/health/2013/04/08/176225511/listen-up-to-smarter-smaller-hearing-aidshttp://www.asha.org/public/hearing/Types-of-Hearing-Aid-Technology/

Hampton, K. N., Goulet, L. S., Rainie, L., & Purcell, K. (2011). *Social networking sites and our lives*. Pew Research Center's Internet & American Life Project. Retrieved June 17, 2014 from http://pewinternet.org/~/media/Files/Reports/2011/PIP%20-%20Social%20networking%20sites%20and%20our%20lives.pdf

Harris, M. B. (1994). Growing old gracefully: Age concealment and gender. *Journal of Gerontology: Psychological Sciences*, *48*, P149–P158.

Hartley, D., Rochtchina, E., Newall, P., Golding, M., & Mitchell, P. (2010). Use of hearing aids and assistive listening devices in an older Australian population. *Journal of the American Academy of Audiology*, *21*, 642–653.

Hawkins, K., Pernarelli, J., Ozminkowski, R. J., Bai, M., Gaston, S. J., Hommer, C. ..., & Yeh, C. S. (2011). The prevalence of urinary incontinence and its burden on the quality of life among older adults with medicare supplement insurance. *Quality of Life Research*, *20*, 723–732. doi: 10.1007/s11136-010-9808-0

Hayslip, B., Jr., & Kaminski, P. L. (2005). Grandparents raising their grandchildren: A review of the literature and suggestions for practice. *Gerontologist*, *45*, 262–269.

Heckhausen, J. (1997). Developmental regulation across adulthood: Primary and secondary control of age-related changes. *Developmental Psychology*, *33*, 176–187.

Heckhausen, J., & Schulz, R. (1995). A life-span theory of control. *Psychological Review*, *102*, 284–304.

Hill, R. D. (2005). *Positive aging: A guide for mental health professionals and consumers*. New York: W.W. Norton.

Horn, J. L., & Cattell, R. B. (1967). Age difference in fluid and crystallized intelligence. *Acta Psychologica*, *26*, 107–129.

Horn, J. L., & Donaldson, G. (1976). On the myth of intellectual decline in adulthood. *American Psychologist*, *31*, 701–719.

Hummert, M. L., Garstka, T. A., Shaner, J. L., & Strahm, S. (1994). Stereotypes of the elderly held by young, middle-aged, and elderly adults. *Journal of Gerontology: Psychological Sciences*, *49*, P240–P249.

Hurd Clarke, L., & Griffin, M. (2008). Visible and invisible ageing: Beauty work as a response to ageism. *Ageing & Society*, *28*, 653–674. doi:10.1017/S0144686X07007003

Hyde, Z., Flicker, L., Hankey, G. J., Almeida, O. P., McCaul, K. A., Chubb, S. A. P., & Yeap, B. B. (2010). Prevalence of sexual activity and associated factors in men aged 75 to 95 years. *Annals of Internal Medicine*, *153*, 693–702.

IIHS (Insurance Institute for Highway Safety). (2014). *Q & A: Older drivers.* Retrieved April 18, 2014 from http://www.iihs.org/iihs/topics/t/older-drivers/qanda

Issacowitz, D. D. (2012). Mood regulation in real time: Age differences in the role of looking. *Current Directions in Psychological Science*, *21*, 237–242.

Jacoby, L. L., & Rhodes, M. G. (2006). False remembering in the aged. *Current Directions in Psychological Science*, *15*, 49–53.

Jahn, D. R., Cukrowicz, K. C., Linton, K., & Prabhu, F. (2011). The mediating effect of perceived burdensomeness on the relation between depressive symptoms and suicide ideation in a community sample of older adults. *Aging & Mental Health*, *15*, 214–220. doi: 10.1080/13607863.2010.501064

Jeste, D. V., Ardelt, M., Blazer, D., Craemer, H. C., Vaillant, G., & Meeks, T. M. (2010). Expert Consensus on characteristics of wisdom: A Delphi Method study. *The Gerontologist*, *50*, 668–680. doi:10.1093/geront/gnq022

Joanisse, M., Gagnon, S., & Voloaca, M. (2012). Overly cautious and dangerous: An empirical evidence of the older driver stereotypes. *Accident Analysis and Prevention*, *45*, 802–810. doi: 10.1016/j.aap.2011.11.00

Johnson, M. M. S. (1990). Age differences in decision making: A process methodology for examining strategic information processing. *Journal of Gerontology: Psychological Sciences*, *45*, P75–P78.

Kaplan, M. S., Huguet, N., McFarland, B. H., & Mandle, J. A. (2012). Factors associated with suicide by firearm among U.S. older adult men. *Psychology of Men and Masculinity*, *13*, 65–74. doi: 10.1037/a0023173

Karel, M. J., Gatz, M., & Smyer, M. A. (2012). Aging and mental health in the decade ahead: What psychologists need to know. *American Psychologist*, *67*, 184–198.

Karraker, A., DeLamater, J., & Schwartz, C. R. (2011). Sexual frequency decline from midlife to later life. *The Journals of Gerontology, Series B: Psychological Sciences and Social Sciences*, *66B*, 502–512. doi: 10.1093/geronb/gbr058

Kastenbaum, R. (1999). Dying and bereavement. In J. C. Cavanaugh & S. K. Whitbourne (Eds.), *Gerontology: An interdisciplinary perspective* (pp. 155–186). New York: Oxford University Press.

Kastenbaum, R. (2006). Suicide. In R. Schulz (Ed.), *The encyclopedia of aging* (4th ed.) ( pp. 1155–1156). New York: Springer.

Kausler, D. H., Kausler, B. C., & Krupshaw, J. A. (2007). *The essential guide to aging in the twenty-first century*. Columbia: University of Missouri Press.

Kelly, A., Conell-Price, J., Covinsky, K., Cenzer, I. S., Chang, A., Boscardin, W. J., & Smith, A. K. (2010). Length of stay for older adults residing in nursing homes at the end of life. *Journal of the American Geriatrics Society, 58*, 1701–1706. doi: 10.1111/j.1532-5415.2010.03005.x

Kemper, S. (1994). Elderspeak: Speech accommodations to older adults. *Aging and Cognition, 1*, 17–28.

Kemper, S., & Harden, T. (1999). Experimentally disentangling what's beneficial about elderspeak from what's not. *Psychology and Aging, 14*, 656–670.

Kirchheimer, S. (2013, June). The $8,000 vacuum. *AARP Bulletin, 54*(5), 28.

Kim, J. G., Goldman, A. J., & Biederman, I. (2008). Blind or deaf? A matter of aesthetics. *Perception, 37*, 949–950. doi:10.1068/p5913

Kite, M. E., Stockdale, G. D., Whitley, B. E., Jr., & Johnson, B. T. (2005). Attitudes toward younger and older adults: An updated meta-analytic review. *Journal of Social Issues, 61*, 241–266.

Kivnick, H. Q., & Sinclair, H. M. (1996). Grandparenthood. In J. E. Birren (Ed.), *Encyclopedia of gerontology: Age, aging, and the aged* (Vol. 1, pp. 611–623). San Diego: Academic Press.

Knight, B. G. (2004). *Psychotherapy with older adults* (3rd ed.). Thousand Oaks, CA: Sage.

Knight, B. G., Kaskie, B., Shurgot, G. R., & Dave, J. (2006). Improving the mental health of older adults. In J. E. Birren & K. W. Schaie (Eds.), *Handbook of the psychology of aging* (6th ed.) (pp. 407–424). Boston: Elsevier Academic Press.

Korkki, P. (2013, May 14). Filling up an empty nest. *New York Times*. Retrieved April 18, 2014 from http://www.nytimes.com/2013/05/15/business/retirementspecial/some-older-adults-are-adopting-children.html?pagewanted=all&_r=0

Korte, J., Bohlmeijer, E. T., Westerhof, G. J., & Pot, A. M. (2011). Reminiscence and adaptation to critical life events in older adults with mild to moderate depressive symptoms. *Aging & Mental Health, 15*, 638–646. doi: 10.1080/13607863.2010.551338

Lachman, M. E. (2006). Perceived control over age-related declines: Adaptive beliefs and behaviors. *Current Directions in Psychological Science, 15*, 282–286.

Lang, F. R., & Carstensen, L. L. (1994). Close emotional relationships in late life: Further support for proactive aging in the social domain. *Psychology and Aging, 9*, 315–324.

Lang, F. R., Staudinger, U. M., & Carstensen, L. L. (1998). Perspectives on socioemotional selectivity in late life: How personality and social context do (and do not) make a difference. *Journal of Gerontology: Psychological Sciences, 53B*, P21–P30.

Langer, E. J., & Rodin, J. (1976). The effects of choice and enhanced personal responsibility for the aged: A field experiment in an institutional setting. *Journal of Personality and Social Psychology, 34*, 191–198.

Levenson, R. W., Carstensen, L. L., & Gottman, J. M. (1993). Long-term marriage: Age, gender, and satisfaction. *Psychology and Aging, 8,* 301–313.

Levin, C. A., Wei, W., Akincigil, A., Lucas, J., Bilder, S., & Crystal, S. (2007). Prevalence and treatment of diagnosed depression among elderly nursing home residents in Ohio. *Journal of the American Medical Directors Association, 8,* 585–594. doi: 10.1016/j.jamda.2007.07.010

Levy, B. (1996). Improving memory in old age through implicit self-stereotyping. *Journal of Personality and Social Psychology, 71,* 1092–1107.

Levy, B. R., Slade, M., Kunkel, S., & Kasl, S. (2002). Longitudinal benefit of positive self-perceptions of aging on functioning health. *Journal of Personality and Social Psychology, 83,* 261–270.

Levy, B. R., Zonderman, A. B., Slade, M. D., & Ferrucci, L. (2009). Age stereotypes held earlier in life predict cardiovascular events in later life. *Psychological Science, 20,* 296–298.

Levy, B. R., Zonderman, A. B., Slade, M. D., & Ferrucci, L. (2012). Memory shaped by age stereotypes over time. *The Journals of Gerontology: Series B: Psychological and Social Sciences, 67,* 432–436.

Lin, R. R., Thorpe, R., Gordon-Salant, S., & Ferrucci, L. (2011). Hearing loss prevalence and risk factors among older adults in the United States. *Journal of Gerontology: Medical Sciences, 66A,* 582–590.

Lindau, S. T., Schumm, L. P., Laumann, E. O., Levinson, W., O'Muircheartaigh, C. A., & Waite, L. J. (2007). A study of sexuality and health among older adults in the United States. *New England Journal of Medicine, 357,* 762–774.

Lloyd-Williams, M., Kennedy, V., Sixsmith, A., & Sixsmith, J. (2007). The end of life: A qualitative study of the perceptions of people over the age of 80 on issues surrounding death and dying. *Journal of Pain and Symptom Management, 34,* 60–66.

Löckenhoff, C. E., & Carstensen, L. L. (2007). Age, emotion, and health-related decision strategies: Motivational manipulations can reduce age differences. *Psychology and Aging, 22,* 134–146.

MacBride, M. B., Rhodes, D. J., & Shuster, L. T. (2010). Vulvovaginalatrophy. *Mayo Clinic Proceedings, 85,* 87–94.

Maer, P. (2011). When did Ronald Reagan have Alzheimer's? The debate goes on. *CBS News.* Retrieved April 18, 2014 from http://www.cbsnews.com/8301-503544_162-20030791-503544.html

Mak, W., & Carpenter, B. D. (2007). Humor comprehension in older adults. *Journal of the International Neuropsychological Society, 13,* 606–614. DOI: 10.10170S1355617707070750

Markus, H. R., & Herzog, A. R. (1991). The role of the self-concept in aging. In K. W. Schaie & M. P. Lawton (Eds.), *Annual review of gerontology and geriatrics* (Vol. 11, pp. 110–143). New York: Springer.

Marottoli, R. A. (2007). *Enhancement of driving performance among older drivers.* Retrieved April 25, 2014 from AAA Foundation for Traffic Safety website: https://www.aaafoundation.org/sites/default/files/EnhancingSeniorDrivingPerfReport.pdf

Matthews, F. E., Arthur, A., Barnes, L. E., Bond, J., Jagger, C., Robinson, L., & Brayne, E. (2013). A two-decade comparison of prevalence of dementia in individuals aged 65 years and older from three geographical areas of England: Results of the Cognitive Function and Ageing Study I and II. *The Lancet, 382,* 1405–1412. doi: 10.1016/S0140-6736(13)61570-6

Mayhew, D. R., Simpson, H. M., & Ferguson, S. A. (2006). Collisions involving senior drivers: High-risk conditions and locations. *Traffic Injury Prevention, 7,* 117–124.

McCrae, R. R. (2002). The maturation of personality psychology: Adult personality development and psychological well-being. *Journal of Research in Personality, 36,* 307–317.

McCrae, R. R., & Costa, P. T., Jr. (1987). Validation of the five-factor model of personality across instruments and observers. *Journal of Personality and Social Psychology, 52,* 81–90.

McCrae, R. R., & Costa, P. T., Jr. (1997). Personality trait structure as a human universal. *American Psychologist, 52,* 509–516.

McIlwain, J. K. (2012). *Housing in America: The baby boomers turn 65.* Urban Land Institute. Retrieved April 18, 2014 from http://www.uli.org/wp-content/uploads/ULI-Documents/HousingInAmericaFIN.pdf

McIntosh, W. D., Locker, Jr., L., Briley, K., Ryan, R., & Scott, A. J. (2011). What do older adults seek in their potential romantic partners? Evidence from online personal ads. *International Journal of Aging and Human Development, 72,* 67–82.

McKnight, A. J., & McKnight, A. S. (1993). The effect of cellular phone use upon driver attention. *Accident Analysis and Prevention, 25,* 259–265.

MetLife Foundation/Civic Ventures. (2011). *Encore career choices: Purpose, passion and a paycheck in a tough economy.* Retrieved April 21, 2014 from http://www.encore.org/files/EncoreCareerChoices.pdf

MetLife Mature Market Institute. (2011). *The MetLife study of elder financial abuse: Crimes of occasion, desperation, and predation against America's elders.* New York, NY: Author. Retrieved June 17, 2014 from https://www.metlife.com/assets/cao/mmi/publications/studies/2011/mmi-elder-financial-abuse.pdf

MetLife Mature Market Institute. (2012). *Market survey of long-term care costs: The 2012 Metlife market survey of nursing home, assisted living, adult day services, and home care costs.* Retrieved April 18, 2014 from https://www.metlife.com/assets/cao/mmi/publications/studies/2012/studies/mmi-2012-market-survey-long-term-care-costs.pdf

Meyer, B. J. F., Russo, C., & Talbot, A. (1995). Discourse comprehension and problem solving: Decisions about the treatment of breast cancer by women across the life-span. *Psychology and Aging, 10,* 84–103.

Meyer, B. J. F., Talbot, A. P., & Ranalli, C. (2007). Why older adults make more immediate treatment decisions about cancer than younger adults. *Psychology and Aging, 22,* 505–524.

Miret, M., Nuevo, R., Morant, C., Sainz-Corton, E., Jimenez-Arriero, M. A., Lopez-Ibor, J. ..., & Ayuso-Mateos, J. L. (2010). Differences between younger and older adults in the structure of suicidal intent and its correlates. *The American Journal of Geriatric Psychiatry, 18*, 839–847.

Mojtabai, R., & Olfson, M. (2004). Major depression in community-dwelling middle-aged and older adults: Prevalence and 2- and 4-year follow up symptoms. *Psychological Medicine, 34*, 623–634. doi: 10.1017/S0033291703001764

Morrow-Howell, N. (2006). Volunteerism. In R. Schulz (Ed.), *The encyclopedia of aging* (4th ed.) (pp. 1217–1219). New York: Springer.

Moscicki, E. K., O'Carroll, P., Rae, S. S., Locke, B. Z., Roy, A., & Regier, D., A. (1988). Suicide attempts in the Epidemiologic Catchment Area Study. *The Yale Journal of Biology and Medicine, 61*, 259–268.

Murphey, D., Cooper, M., & Moore, K. A. (2012). *Children living with and cared for by grandparents: State-level data from the American Community Survey.* (Publication No. 2012-31). Child Trends Research Brief. Retrieved April 18, 2014 from http://www.childtrends.org/wp-content/uploads/2012/10/Child_Trends-2012_10_01_RB_Grandchildren.pdf

Murphy, S. L., Xu, J., & Kochanek, K. D. (2013). Deaths: Final data for 2010. *National Vital Statistics Reports, 61*(4). Retrieved April 18, 2014 from http://www.cdc.gov/nchs/data/nvsr/nvsr61/nvsr61_04.pdf

National Association for Shoplifting Prevention. (n.d.). *Shoplifting statistics.* Retrieved April 18, 2014 from http://www.shopliftingprevention.org/WhatNASPOffers/NRC/PublicEducStats.htm

National Council on Aging. (2013). 47 states celebrate 6th Annual Falls Prevention Awareness Day [Press release]. Retrieved April 29, 2014 from http://www.ncoa.org/press-room/press-release/47-states-celebrate-6th.html

National Institute on Aging, National Institutes of Health. (2013). *Falls and older adults: Causes and risk factors.* Retrieved April 18, 2014 from http://nihseniorhealth.gov/falls/causesandriskfactors/01.html

National Institute on Aging, National Institutes of Health, Alzheimer's Disease Education and Referral Center. (n.d.). *About Alzheimer's disease: Alzheimer's basics.* Retrieved April 18, 2014 from http://www.nia.nih.gov/alzheimers/topics/alzheimers-basics

National Institute on Deafness and Other Communication Disorders. National Institutes of Health. (2001). *Hearing loss and older adults.* Retrieved April 18, 2014 from http://www.nidcd.nih.gov/health/hearing/Pages/older.aspx

National Institute on Deafness and Other Communication Disorders. National Institutes of Health. (2010). *Quick statistics.* Retrieved April 18, 2014 from http://www.nidcd.nih.gov/health/statistics/Pages/quick.aspx

Neff, J. (2013, April 22). Tony Siragusa: The new face of male light bladder leakage. *Advertising Age.* Retrieved April 18, 2014 from http://adage.com/article/news/tony-siragusa-pitches-depend-light-bladder-leakage-line/240969/

Neimeyer, R. A., & Fortner, B. (2006). Death anxiety. In R. Schulz (Ed.), *The encyclopedia of aging* (4th ed.) (pp. 283–284). New York: Springer.

Neugarten, B. L., Havinghurst, R. J., & Tobin, S. (1968). Personality and patterns of aging. In B. L. Neugarten (Ed.), *Middle age and aging* (pp. 173–177). Chicago: University of Chicago Press.

Norris, J. E., & Tindale, J. A. (1994). *Among generations: The cycle of adult relationships*. New York: W. H. Freeman.

Palmore, E. (2001). The ageism survey: First findings. *The Gerontologist, 41*, 572–575.

Panek, P. E. (1997). The older worker. In A. D. Fisk & W. A. Rogers (Eds.), *The handbook of human factors and the older adult* (pp. 363–394). San Diego: Academic Press.

Park, D. C., & Reuter-Lorenz, P. (2009). The adaptive brain: Aging and neurocognitive scaffolding. *Annual Review of Psychology, 60*, 173–196.

Passuth, P. M., & Bengston, V. L. (1988). Sociological theories of aging: Current perspectives and future directions. In J. E. Birren & V. L. Bengston (Eds.), *Emergent theories of aging* (pp. 333–355). New York: Springer.

Perry, E. L., Kulik, C. T., & Bourhis, A. C. (1996). Moderating effects of personal and contextual factors in age discrimination. *Journal of Applied Psychology, 81*, 628–647.

Pew Research Center. (2009). *Growing old in America: Expectations vs. reality*. (Social & Demographic Trends Report. Retrieved April 18, 2014 from http://pewsocialtrends.org/files/2010/10/Getting-Old-in-America.pdf

Pew Research Center. (2010). *The return of the multi-generational family household*. Retrieved April 18, 2014 from http://www.pewsocialtrends.org/2010/03/18/the-return-of-the-multi-generational-family-household/

Pew Research Center. (2011). *Fighting poverty in a tough economy, Americans move in with their relatives*. Retrieved April 18, 2014 from http://www.pewsocialtrends.org/files/2011/10/Multigenerational-Households-Final1.pdf

Pew Research Center. (2013). *Pew Research Center's Internet & American Life Project Spring Tracking Survey 2012, March 15-April 3, 2012* [Crosstab file]. Retrieved April 18, 2014 from http://pewinternet.org/Shared-Content/Data-Sets/2012/April-2012--Cell-Phones.aspx

Pillemer, K. (2011). *30 lessons for living: Tried and true advice from the wisest Americans*. New York: Hudson Street Press.

Pinquart, M., Duberstein, P. R., & Lyness, J. M. (2007). Effects of psychotherapy and other behavioral interventions on clinically depressed older adults: A meta-analysis. *Aging & Mental Health, 11*, 645–657.

Popelka, M. M., Cruickshanks, K. J., Wiley, T. L., Tweed, T. S., Klein, B. E. K., & Klein, R. (1998). Low prevalence of hearing aid use among older adults with hearing loss: The epidemiology of hearing loss study. *Journal of the American Geriatrics Society, 46*, 1075–1078.

Prince Market Research. (2007). *Clarity final report: Attitudes of seniors and baby boomers on aging in place*. Retrieved April 18, 2014 from http://americareinfo.com/site/wp-content/uploads/2009/09/Clarity_Aging_in_Place_2007.pdf

Protecting Older Workers Against Discrimination Act of 2012, S. 2189, 112th Cong. (2012). Retrieved April 18, 2014 from http://www.govtrack.us/congress/bills/112/s2189

Qato, D. M., Alexander, G. C., Conti, R. M., Johnson, M., Schumm, P., & Lindau, S. T. (2008). Use of prescription and over-the-counter medications and dietary supplements among older adults in the United States. *Journal of the American Medical Association, 300*, 2867–2878. doi:10.1001/jama.2008.892

Quinn, J. B. (May, 2013). Choosing the safest path. *AARP Bulletin, 24.*

Reed, A. E., & Carstensen, L. L. (2012). The theory behind the age-related positivity effect. *Frontiers in Psychology, 3,* 1–10. doi: 10.3389/fpsyg.2012.00339

Reitzes, D. C., Mutran, E. J., & Fernandez, M. E. (1998). The decision to retire: A career perspective. *Social Science Quarterly, 79*, 607–619.

Rix, S. E. (2011). Employment and aging. In R. H. Binstock & L. K. George (Eds.), *Handbook of aging and the social sciences* (7th ed.) (pp 193–206). San Diego: Elsevier Academic Press.

Rix, S. E. (2012). *The employment situation, May 2012: Good news is hard to find.* AARP Public Policy Institute Fact Sheet. Retrieved April 18, 2014 from http://www.aarp.org/content/dam/aarp/research/public_policy_institute/econ_sec/2012/the-employment-situation-may-2012-AARP-ppi-econ-sec.pdf

Roberts, B. W., & DelVecchio, W. F. (2000). The rank-order consistency of personality traits from childhood to old age: A quantitative review of longitudinal studies. *Psychological Bulletin, 126*, 3–25. doi: 10.1037//0033-2909.126.I.3

Robinson, T., Callister, M., Magoffin, D., & Moore, J. (2007). The portrayal of older characters in Disney animated films. *Journal of Aging Studies, 21*, 203–213. doi:10.1016/j.jaging.2006.10.001

Rockwood, K. (2006). Vascular cognitive impairment. In R. Schulz (Ed.), *The encyclopedia of aging* (4th ed.) (pp. 1208–1210). New York: Springer.

Roenker, D. L., Cissell, G. M., Ball, K. K., Wadley, V. G., & Edwards, J. D. (2003). Speed-of-processing and driving simulator training result in improved driving performance. *Human Factors, 45*, 218–233.

Rogers, W. A., & Fisk, A. D. (2001). Understanding the role of attention in cognitive aging research. In J. E. Birren & K. W. Schaie (Eds.), *Handbook of the psychology of aging* (5th ed.) (pp. 267–287). San Diego: Academic Press.

Ronald Reagan Presidential Library. (1994, November 5). *Text of letter written by President Ronald Reagan announcing he has Alzheimer's disease.* Retrieved April 18, 2014 from http://www.reagan.utexas.edu/archives/reference/alzheimerletter.html

Rook, K. S. (1987). Reciprocity of social exchange and social satisfaction among older women. *Journal of Personality and Social Psychology, 52*, 145–154.

Ruggles, S. (2007). The decline of intergenerational coresidence in the United States, 1850 to 2000. *American Sociological Review, 72*, 964–989.

Ryan, E. B., Anas, A. P., & Gruneir, A. J. S. (2006). Evaluations of overhelping and underhelping communication. *Journal of Language and Social Psychology, 25*, 97–107.

Ryan, E. B., Hummert, M. L., & Anas, A. P. (1997, November). *The impact of old age and hearing impairment on first impressions.* Paper presented at the Gerontological Society of America Convention, Cincinnati, Ohio.

Ryan, E. B., Hummert, M. L., & Boich, L. H. (1995). Communication predicaments of aging: Patronizing behavior toward older adults. *Journal of Language and Social Psychology, 14*, 144–166.

Sacher, E. (2012, October). The law. *AARP Bulletin, 53*(8), p. 34.

Salthouse, T. A. (2010). *Major issues in cognitive aging*. New York: Oxford University Press.

Salthouse, T. A., & Maurer, T. J. (1996). Aging, job performance, and career development. In J. E. Birren, & K. W. Schaie (Eds.), *Handbook of the psychology of aging* (4th ed.) (pp. 353–364). San Diego: Academic Press.

Sanofi-Aventis. (2013). *Ambien CR® Prescribing Information*. Retrieved April 18, 2014 from http://products.sanofi.us/ambien_cr/ambienCR.html

Schaie, K. W. (1965). A general model for the study of developmental problems. *Psychological Bulletin, 64*, 92–107.

Schaie, K. W. (1994). The course of adult intellectual development. *American Psychologist, 49*, 304–313.

Scheffer, A. C., Schuurmans, J. J., van Dijk, N., van der Hooft, T., & de Rooij, S. E. (2008). Fear of falling: Measurement strategy, prevalence, risk factors and consequences among older persons. *Age and Ageing, 37*, 19–24. doi: 10.1093/ageing/afm169

Scheibe, S. (2012). The golden years of emotion. *Observer, 25*(9), 19–21.

Schneider, B. A., & Pichora-Fuller, M. K. (2000). Implications of perceptual deterioration for cognitive aging research. In F. I. M. Craik & T. A. Salthouse (Eds.), *The handbook of aging and cognition* (2nd ed.) (pp. 155–219). Mahwah, NJ: Erlbaum.

Schulz, R. (1976). The effects of control and predictability on the psychological and physical well-being of the institutionalized aged. *Journal of Personality and Social Psychology, 33*, 563–573.

Schulz, R., & Heckhausen, J. (1996). A life span model of successful aging. *American Psychologist, 51*, 702–714.

Schuman, I. (2013, July 31). *Protecting older workers against discrimination act reintroduced in both chambers*. Littler Workplace Policy Institute. Retrieved April 29, 2014 from http://www.littler.com/dc-employment-law-update/protecting-older-workers-against-discrimination-act-reintroduced-both-chamb

Schwartz, K. (2013, July 31). Seeking a "middle-aged" look. *New York Times*. Retrieved April 18, 2014 from http://www.nytimes.com/2013/08/01/fashion/seeking-a-middle-aged-look.html?_r=0

Sekuler, A. B., Bennett, P. J., & Mamelak, M. (2000). Effects of aging on the useful field of view. *Experimental Aging Research, 26*, 103–120.

Seltzer, J. A., Lau, C. Q., & Bianchi, S. M. (2012). Doubling up when times are tough: A study of obligations to share a home in response to economic hardship. *Social Science Research, 41*, 1307–1309.

Senator Tom Harkin. (2012). Bipartisan legislation will protect older workers from discrimination [Press release]. Retrieved April 18, 2014 from http://www.harkin.senate.gov/press/release.cfm?i=336287

Shabsigh, R. (2006). Epidemiology of erectile dysfunction. In J. J. Mulcahy (Ed.), *Current clinical urology: Male sexual function: A guide to clinical management* (2nd ed.) Totowa, NJ: Humana Press.

Shadel, D. (2012, October/November). Confessions of a scam artist. *AARP Magazine*, pp. 63–65.

Shanas, E. (1979). Social myth as hypothesis: The case of the family relations of old people. *Gerontologist, 19*, 3–9.

Sharit, J., Czaja, S. J., Hernandez, M., Yang, Y., Perdomo, D., Lewis, J. E. …, & Nair, S. (2004). An evaluation of performance by older persons on a simulated telecommunicating task. *Journal of Gerontology: Psychological Sciences, 59B*, P305–P316.

Siegler, I. C., & Botwinick, J. (1979). A long-term longitudinal study of intellectual ability of older adults: The matter of selective subject attrition. *Journal of Gerontology, 34*, 242–245.

Sievert, K. D., Amend, B., Toomey, P. A., Robinson, D., Milsom, I., Koelbl, H., & Newman, D. K. (2012). Can we prevent incontinence?: ICI-RS 2011. *Neurology and Urodynamics, 31*, 390–399. doi: 10.1002/nau.22225

Silcoff, M. (2013, April 26). Why your grandpa is cooler than you. *New York Times*. Retrieved April 18, 2014 from http://www.nytimes.com/2013/04/28/magazine/why-your-grandpa-is-cooler-than-you.html?pagewanted=all

Silverthorne, Z. A., & Quinsey, V. L. (2000). Sexual partner age preferences of homosexual and heterosexual men and women. *Archives of Sexual Behavior, 29*, 67–76.

Sims, J., Browning, C., Lundgren-Lindquist, B., & Kendig, H. (2011). Urinary incontinence in a community sample of older adults: Prevalence and impact on quality of life. *Disability and Rehabilitation, 33*, 1389–1398. doi: 10.3109/09638288.2010.532284

Skoog, I., Blennow, K., & Marcusson, J. (1996). Dementia. In J. E. Birren (Ed.), *Encyclopedia of gerontology: Age, aging, and the aged* (Vol. 1, pp. 383–403). San Diego: Academic Press.

Smith, A. (2013). *Smartphone ownership – 2013 update.* Pew Research Center's Internet & American Life Project. Retrieved April 21, 2014 from http://pewinternet.org/~/media//Files/Reports/2013/PIP_Smartphone_adoption_2013.pdf

Smith, J., & Baltes, P. B. (1990). Wisdom-related knowledge: Age/cohort differences in response to life-planning problems. *Developmental Psychology, 26*, 494–505.

Smith, J., & Freund, A. M. (2002). The dynamics of possible selves in old age. *Journal of Gerontology: Psychological Sciences, 57B*, P492–P500.

Smith, J., Staudinger, U. M., & Baltes, P. B. (1994). Occupational settings facilitating wisdom-related knowledge: The sample case of clinical psychologists. *Journal of Consulting and Clinical Psychology, 62*, 989–999.

Snowden, J. S., Neary, D., & Mann, M. A. (2002). Frontotemporal dementia. *British Journal of Psychiatry, 180*, 140–143. doi: 10.1192/bjp.180.2.140

Snowdon, D. A. (1997). Aging and Alzheimer's disease: Lessons from the Nun Study. *Gerontologist, 37*, 150–156.

Sontag, S. (1972, September 23). The double standard of aging. *Saturday Review*, *29–38*.

Staudinger, U. M., & Bowen, C. E. (2010). Life-span perspectives on positive personality development in adulthood and old age. In M. E. Lamb and A. M. Freund (Eds.), *The handbook of life-span development. Vol. 2: Social and emotional development* (pp. 254–297). Hoboken, NJ, John Wiley & Sons, Inc.

Stein, E. (2003). When is hypochondriasis not hypochondriasis? *Geriatrics*, *58*, 41–42.

Sternberg, R. J., & Lubart, T. I. (2001). Wisdom and creativity. In J. E. Birren & K. W. Schaie (Eds.), *Handbook of the psychology of aging* (5th ed.) (pp. 500–522). San Diego: Academic Press.

Sterns, A. A., & Sterns, H. L. (1997). Should there be an affirmative action policy for hiring older persons? Yes. In A. E. Scharlach & L. W. Kaye (Eds.), *Controversial issues in aging* (pp. 35–39). Boston: Allyn & Bacon.

Stevens, A. (1994). *Jung*. New York: Oxford University Press.

Stoller, E. P., & Longino, C. F., Jr. (2001). "Going home" or "leaving home"? The impact of person and place ties on anticipated counterstream migration. *Gerontologist*, *41*, 96–102.

Swarns, R. (2012, March 1). More Americans rejecting marriage in 50s and beyond. *The New York Times*. Retrieved April 18, 2014 from http://www.nytimes.com/2012/03/02/us/more-americans-rejecting-marriage-in-50s-and-beyond.html?pagewanted=all&_r=0

Taranto, M. A. (1989). Facets of wisdom: A theoretical synthesis. *International Journal of Aging and Human Development*, *29*, 1–21.

Teno, J. M., Gozalo, P. L., Bynum, J. P. W., Leland, N. E., Miller, S. C., Morden, S. E. ..., & Mor, V. (2013). Change in end-of-life care for Medicare beneficiaries: Site of death, place of care, and health care transitions in 2000, 2005, and 2009. *Journal of the American Medical Association*, *309*, 470–477. doi:10.1001/jama.2012.207624

Teuscher, U., & Teuscher C. (2007). Reconsidering the double standard of aging: Effects of gender and sexual orientation on facial attractiveness ratings. *Personality and Individual Differences*, *42*, 631–639.

Thomas, J. L. (1990). The grandparent role: A double bind. *International Journal of Aging and Human Development*, *31*, 169–177.

Thomas, P. A. (2010). Is it better to give or to receive? Social support and the well-being of older adults. *Journal of Gerontology: Social Sciences*, *65B*, 351–357, doi:10.1093/geronb/gbp113.

Thorson, J. A., & Powell, F. C. (2000). Death anxiety in young and older adults. In A. Tomer (Ed.), *Death attitudes and the older adult: Theories, concepts, and applications* (pp. 123–136). Philadelphia: Brunner-Routledge.

Towers Watson. (2012). *Global workforce study*. Retrieved April 18, 2014 from http://towerswatson.com/assets/pdf/2012-Towers-Watson-Global-Workforce-Study.pdf

Tucker, J. S., Wingard, D. L., Friedman, H. S., & Schwartz, J. W. (1996). Marital history at midlife as a predictor of longevity: Alternative explanations to the protective effect of marriage. *Health Psychology, 15*, 94–101.

U.S. Census Bureau. (2012). *Statistical Abstract of the United States*. P. 688, Transportation. Retrieved April 18, 2014 from http://www.census.gov/compendia/statab/2012/tables/12s1114.pdf

U.S. Department of Health and Human Services, Administration on Aging, Administration for Community Living. (2012). *A Profile of Older Americans: 2012*. Retrieved April 18, 2014 from http://www.aoa.gov/Aging_Statistics/Profile/2012/docs/2012profile.pdf

U.S. Food and Drug Administration. (2012). *Important safety label changes to cholesterol-lowering statin drugs*. [FDA drug safety communication]. Retrieved April 18, 2014 from http://www.fda.gov/drugs/drugsafety/ucm293101.htm#sa

Visual Awareness Research Group, Inc. (2009). *UFOV® User's Guide*. Retrieved April 18, 2014 from http://crag.uab.edu/VAI/PDF%20Pubs/UFOV_Manual_V6.1.4.pdf

Wagman, M. (1983). A factor analytic study of the psychological implications of the computer for the individual and society. *Behavior Research Methods & Instrumentation, 15*, 413–419.

Waite, L. J., Laumann, E. O., Das, A., & Schumm, L. P. (2009). Sexuality: Measures of partnerships, practices, attitudes, and problems in the National Social Life, Health, and Aging Study. *Journal of Gerontology: Social Sciences, 64B*, i56–i66, doi:10.1093/geronb/gbp038

Watson, W. K., & Stelle, C. (2011). Dating for older women: Experiences and meanings of dating in later life. *Journal of Women and Aging, 23*, 263–275. doi: 10.1080/08952841.2011.587732

Watson, L. C., Lebmann, S., Mayer, L., Samus, Q., Baker, A., Brandt, J., & Lyketsos, C. (2006). Depression in assisted living is common and related to physical burden. *The American Journal of Geriatric Psychiatry, 14*, 876–883.

Wei, W., Sambamoorthi, U., Olfson, J., Walkup, J. T., & Crystal, S. (2005). Use of psychotherapy for depression in older adults. *The American Journal of Psychiatry, 162*, 711–717.

Whitehouse, P. J. (2007). Dementia: Alzheimer's. In J. E. Birren (Ed.), *Encyclopedia of gerontology: Age, aging, and the aged* (2nd ed.) (Vol. 1, pp. 374–379). Boston: Elsevier Academic Press.

Widrick, R. M., & Raskin, J. D. (2010). Age-related stigma and the golden section hypothesis. *Aging and Mental Health, 14*, 375–385. doi: 10.1080/13607860903167846

Wingfield, A., & Stine-Morrow, E. A. L. (2000). Language and speech. In F. I. M. Craik & T. A. Salthouse (Eds.), *Handbook of aging and cognition* (2nd ed.) (pp. 359–416). Mahwah, NJ: Erlbaum.

Wingfield, A., Tun, P. A., & McCoy, S. L. (2005). Hearing loss in older adulthood: What it is and how it interacts with cognitive performance. *Current Directions in Psychological Science, 14*, 144–148.

Winik, M. (2013, August–September). Single and loving it. *AARP The Magazine*, 66–67.

Wink, P., & Scott, J. (2005). Does religiousness buffer against the fear of death and dying in late adulthood? Findings from a longitudinal study. *Journal of Gerontology: Psychological Sciences, 60B*, P207–P214.

Woodruff-Pak, D. S. (1989). Aging and intelligence: Changing perspectives in the twentieth century. *Journal of Aging Studies, 3*, 91–118.

Yardley, L., Donovan-Hall, M., Francis, K., & Todd, C. (2006). Older people's views of advice about falls prevention: A qualitative study. *Health Education Research Theory and Practice, 21*, 509–517. doi:10.1093/her/cyh077

# INDEX

*Great Myths of Aging*, First Edition. Joan T. Erber and Lenore T. Szuchman.
© 2015 John Wiley & Sons, Inc. Published 2015 by John Wiley & Sons, Inc.

arthritis, 67, 77
assisted living facilities, 91–92,
    96, 102, 119, 128–129
  *see also* caregiving for older
    adults; nursing homes
attitude strength, 89–90
attractiveness
  beauty work, cosmetic
    procedures, 25–29
  "double standard of aging,"
    26–29
Ayers, C. R., 96–97

Bacon, C. G., 23
Ball, K. K., 18
Baltes, P. B., 38, 39–40, 56, 58
Barry, K. L., 134
Barsky, A. J., 69
Bengston, V. L., 82, 99,
    106, 107, 108
bereavement, 90, 106, 126,
    136, 138–139
Bianchi, S. M., 99
Biederman, I., 10
Birditt, K. S., 76
Birren, J. E., 56
bladder control, 20, 29–32
Blennow, K., 47
Blow, F. C., 134
Bluck, S., 57
body, 4–5, 6–36, 67–68, 90, 96
  arthritis, 67, 77
  beauty work, 25–29
  cardiovascular system, 4, 23, 54
  effect of marital status on
    overall health, 32–36
  falls, 13–14
  hearing loss, 6–12, 77
  incontinence, 20, 29–32
  menopausal issues, 22, 23
  prostate problems, 30, 31

and sexual health, 20–24
  vision problems, 18, 19
Bohlmeijer, E. T., 94
Boich, L. H., 9
Botwinick, J., 39, 41
Bourhis, A. C., 111
Bowen, C. E., 3, 4, 109, 117
brain-imaging research, 49, 62
Braithwaite, V. A., 73
Braitman, K. A., 16
Braver, E. R., 16
breast cancer, 23
Briley, K., 127
Brockman, L. M., 134
Brown, S. L., 35
Browning, C., 30
Burton, L., 99
Buss, D. M., 27–28
Butler, R. N., 49

Caine, E. D., 132, 133
Callister, M., 75
cancer survivors, 23
Cantor, M., 107
capacity (mental capacity),
    25, 53
cardiovascular system, 4, 23, 54
caregiving for older adults,
    32–33, 53, 70, 101–102,
    106–108, 126, 127,
    130, 138
  childcare by older adults,
    103–104, 116
  *see also* assisted living
    facilities; nursing homes
Carstensen, L. L., 34, 63,
    64, 76, 83–84, 85
Castle, E., 62
Cattell, R. B., 39
cautiousness, 63–65
cell phones, 44–45

frontotemporal dementia
(FTD), 52
Fry, P. S., 137
funerals, 136
Fung, H. H., 83, 84–85

Gartska, T. A., 74
Gatz, M., 50, 51, 93
Giarrusso, R., 104
Glück, J., 57
Gold, D. T., 107, 137
Goldman, A. J., 10
Gorden-Salant, S., 9
Gottman, J. M., 34, 76
Goulet, L. S., 45
grandchildren, 44, 94,
98–105, 116
Greendale, G. A., 79
Griffin, M., 26, 27
Grodstein, F., 49
Gross, J. J., 76, 83
grouchiness, 66–67, 75–77
Gruenewald, T. L., 79
Gruley, B., 24–25
Gruneir, A. J. S., 9

Haight, B. K., 95
Hamid, E., 46
Hamilton, H., 12
Hampton, K. N., 45
Harden, T., 8–9
Harris, M. B., 27
Havinghurst, R. J., 81
Hawkins, K., 30
Hayslip, B., Jr., 116
healthcare costs, 11–12, 53, 74,
93, 94, 119–120
hearing loss, 6–12, 77
"elderspeak," 8–9
hearing aids, 9–12
incidence, 7

phonemic regression, 8
presbycusis, 7–8
Heckhausen, J., 79
Heindel, W. C., 17
Hendrix, S., 95
Henry, W., 82
Herzog, A. R., 86
hierarchical-compensatory
model (relationships), 107
Hill, R. D., 129, 130
home
accident prevention, 13, 14, 80
migration to/from Sunbelt,
122–123
multi-generational households,
87–88, 98–102, 103–104
Horn, J. L., 39
Hughes, P. C., 125
Huguet, N., 133
Hummert, M. L., 9, 74
Hurd Clarke, L., 26, 27
Hyde, Z., 21
hypochondriasis, 66–71

implicit priming experiments, 3–4
incontinence, 20, 29–32
independent living, 19, 35, 53–54,
79, 80–81, 87, 91
accident prevention, 13, 14, 80
Insurance Institute for Highway
Safety (IIHS), 15–16, 17
intelligence, 37–42
crystallized and fluid abilities, 39
pragmatics of and
mechanics of, 40
intergenerational households,
87–88, 98–102, 103–104
Internet use, 44–46, 100,
126–127
introversion, 81–85
IQ (intelligence quotient), 37–42